HENRY FORD

A HEARTHSIDE PERSPECTIVE

Other SAE books of interest:

Edsel Ford and E.T. Gregorie
The Remarkable Design Team and
Their Classic Fords of the 1930s and 1940s
by Henry Dominguez
(Order No. R-245)

The Birth of Chrysler Corporation and
Its Engineering Legacy
by Carl Breer
Edited by Anthony J. Yanik
(Order No. R-144)

For more information or to order these books, contact SAE at 400 Commonwealth Drive, Warrendale, PA 15096-0001; (724) 776-4970; fax (724) 776-0790; e-mail: publications@sae.org.

HENRY FORD

A HEARTHSIDE PERSPECTIVE

DONN P. WERLING

Society of Automotive Engineers, Inc.
Warrendale, Pa.

Library of Congress Cataloging-in-Publication Data

Werling, Donn Paul.
  Henry Ford : a hearthside perspective / Donn P. Werling.
    p. cm.
  Includes bibliographical references and index.
  ISBN 0-7680-0456-X
  1. Ford, Henry, 1863-1947. 2. Businesspeople--United States--Biography.
  3. Automobile industry and trade--United States. I. Title.

HD9710.U52 F6685 2000
338.7'6292'092--dc21
[B]   99-086824

Copyright © 2000   Society of Automotive Engineers, Inc.
                    400 Commonwealth Drive
                    Warrendale, PA 15096-0001 U.S.A.
                    Phone: (724) 776-4841
                    Fax: (724) 776-5760
                    E-mail: publications@sae.org
                    http://www.sae.org

ISBN 0-7680-0456-X

SAE Order No. R-266

Cover photo: *Henry Ford at the hearthside of his 1836 Botsford Inn in Farmington, Michigan, by W.E. Vice, 1925. The Botsford Inn was restored by Ford in 1924. (From the Collections of the Henry Ford Estate, University of Michigan–Dearborn.)*

TABLE OF CONTENTS

This book is dedicated to the docents and volunteers
of the Henry Ford Estate—Fair Lane

FOREWORD

This book is a wonderful collection of interesting information and is presented in a fascinating manner. I've learned a lot about Henry Ford which I had failed to recognize prior to reading the book. The unique association of the usual facts, with musings and songs, deserves a medium of presentation beyond merely that of an ordinary printed book. It has the elements of a play or musical. A CD and school musicale entitled "Henry Ford and His Uncommon Friends" has been produced to enthusiastic reviews using these songs.

I followed the story easily and found it tremendously interesting. Use of the timeline and chapter headings will help the reader to follow the story of the life of Henry Ford. To completely explain Henry Ford in a few hundred pages is, of course, impossible, but the author has revealed in this book many of Henry's most salient attributes in a delightful manner. Although unorthodox in composition, the book surely will reward the reader.

This book was a joy for me to read. There is potential, I believe, for this new and engaging style of presentation.

Ford Bryan

Ford Bryan is the author of:
Beyond the Model T
The Fords of Dearborn
Henry's Lieutenants
Henry's Attic

FORD MILESTONES

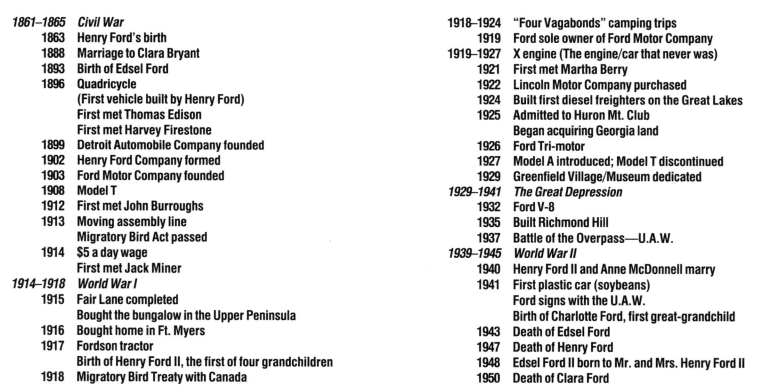

1861–1865	*Civil War*
1863	Henry Ford's birth
1888	Marriage to Clara Bryant
1893	Birth of Edsel Ford
1896	Quadricycle
	(First vehicle built by Henry Ford)
	First met Thomas Edison
	First met Harvey Firestone
1899	Detroit Automobile Company founded
1902	Henry Ford Company formed
1903	Ford Motor Company founded
1908	Model T
1912	First met John Burroughs
1913	Moving assembly line
	Migratory Bird Act passed
1914	$5 a day wage
	First met Jack Miner
1914–1918	*World War I*
1915	Fair Lane completed
	Bought the bungalow in the Upper Peninsula
1916	Bought home in Ft. Myers
1917	Fordson tractor
	Birth of Henry Ford II, the first of four grandchildren
1918	Migratory Bird Treaty with Canada

1918–1924	"Four Vagabonds" camping trips
1919	Ford sole owner of Ford Motor Company
1919–1927	X engine (The engine/car that never was)
1921	First met Martha Berry
1922	Lincoln Motor Company purchased
1924	Built first diesel freighters on the Great Lakes
1925	Admitted to Huron Mt. Club
	Began acquiring Georgia land
1926	Ford Tri-motor
1927	Model A introduced; Model T discontinued
1929	Greenfield Village/Museum dedicated
1929–1941	*The Great Depression*
1932	Ford V-8
1935	Built Richmond Hill
1937	Battle of the Overpass—U.A.W.
1939–1945	*World War II*
1940	Henry Ford II and Anne McDonnell marry
1941	First plastic car (soybeans)
	Ford signs with the U.A.W.
	Birth of Charlotte Ford, first great-grandchild
1943	Death of Edsel Ford
1947	Death of Henry Ford
1948	Edsel Ford II born to Mr. and Mrs. Henry Ford II
1950	Death of Clara Ford

ACKNOWLEDGMENTS

First, I wish to thank the University of Michigan–Dearborn and my many colleagues from the Chancellor downward, who are dedicated to the value of truth and research for what that truth might be. For my position and the support of the position of the directorship of the Henry Ford Estate as a National Historic Landmark, I am indeed grateful.

Second, I would like to thank the many volunteers from the community who have given so much of their time and money over these many years to place this landmark on the restoration track, and as guides, interpreters, and receptionists have opened it to the public. Similar to Jefferson's Monticello, the restoration of Fair Lane has been and continues to be a challenge. Henry Ford did not believe in endowments. Furthermore, the Estate is complex and the needs are great. Therefore, like Monticello, Fair Lane probably will require a hundred years in which to find all or most of the furniture and to restore it and the home to a status that is truly representative of what once was.

Third, I would like to thank the following individuals. Robert Behrens, Vice Chancellor for Business Affairs, encouraged the writing of this biography from the onset. Ford Bryan, Edsel B. Ford II, Leslie and Lucy Long, Peggy Campbell (a grandniece of Clara Ford), and Bruce Simpson provided patronage and family ties to the Ford family and worked to make the numerous tasks easier in many ways. Mike Skinner and Dick Folsom each provided corrections to and criticisms of the manuscript in its early versions and are especially to be thanked, as are many of their fellow members of the Henry Ford Heritage Association. John Berger, the Vice President of the Henry Ford Heritage Association, was both a delightful and insightful research associate on my southern research trip in 1997. Ron Weary, a retired Ford Motor Company engineer and fellow Valparaiso alumnus, not only proved to be a great research associate but also helped me see Henry Ford through the eyes of an engineer. Thanks also are extended to Steve Pedler and Jan Habarth for their tireless editorial efforts that greatly improved the quality of the final manuscript.

Finally, I want to thank Diane, my wife of almost 30 years, for the encouragement, support, and inspiration that both she and our son Ben continually provide. I am indebted to Ben particularly for having his perspective as I was writing the living history vignette of young Henry Ford exploring the banks of the Rouge.

Most visitors who come to Fair Lane want to see the powerhouse and residence. A much smaller percentage sees the gardens around the house. As I have often commented to visitors, the Fords had 25 gardeners and 5 household servants. Were that ratio taken as representative of what both Fords truly enjoyed—through winter, spring, summer, and fall—then visitors to the Estate should spend five times as much of their time outdoors as indoors to experience and enjoy Fair Lane as the Fords did.

The Fords loved Michigan for its four-season beauty. Although they could have lived and ended their days anywhere in the world, Fair Lane was their home of choice. They were born and died within its walls or within mere miles of its location. I am thankful that for the last decade and a half, it has been my home and inspiration as well.

Donn P. Werling

Huron Mt. Club

Jack Miner's
Bird Refuge

Wayside Inn

Fair Lane
and the Rouge plant

Berry College

Richmond Hill

Tuskegee Institute

Ft. Myers

Henry Ford's life had a global impact. However, the sites identified here were hearth and home because of the time Henry Ford spent in working, resting, recreating, donating, preserving, building, and restoring. Henry Ford's beloved mother, Mary Litigot Ford, once said that play after work was done was not only well earned but more fun. Although each site has its own unique perspective in relation to Henry Ford's life, Henry Ford mixed in full measures of work and play at each of these hearthsides revisited in this book.

INTRODUCTION

To many who know his life only through recent media coverage, Henry Ford should not even be considered as a role model for future generations. Some people in the film and television industries have labeled him as having been more of a throwback and politically incorrect, both during and after his life. With the current public scrutiny and execution by the media of almost anyone deemed heroic, this sentiment also is found in a great number of books, as the total number of biographies produced on Henry Ford alone is close to 100 or perhaps more. America likes labels. Although Henry Ford once held the label of folk hero, this view has faded in America and in the eyes of the rest of the world, even though interest in the man remains strong.

Nonetheless, it is undeniable that those in charge of deciding what historic home, event, or site is important to our nation's history have already deemed that Henry Ford was one of the great figures of American history. The number of officially designated historic sites affiliated with Henry Ford ranks him at the top of the National Historic Register of Historic Places, along with Abraham Lincoln, the emancipator of slaves, and Washington and Jefferson, both slave owners. Chinese delegations regularly visit the home of Henry Ford in Dearborn, Michigan, with near reverence in an attempt to understand who this great American was. Henry Ford remains as one of the few Americans to have had his biography done in Chinese while he was alive (1929).[i] Some academics at the University of Michigan–Dearborn were rather surprised to learn that the first Russian scholar and Fulbright winner came to the Dearborn campus to study the life of Henry Ford. These examples demonstrate that although Ford has been labeled by some as politically incorrect, even by those in his hometown, the world still comes to hear his story.

Ford was wrong with his anti-Semitic ramblings, which portions of this book trace to a variety of sources. In the politically correct hindsight judgment of history, it is known that Presidents Washington and Jefferson were wrong to own slaves and to exploit them for financial and personal favors as they both did. The point is that all world figures throughout history were simply human beings with feet of clay, and Henry Ford was no exception. His son Edsel, labor unions, and Jews did not always experience fair treatment from Henry, which is widely documented. This book by no means works to absolve those failings. However, the pendulum swings—from truly heroic to tragic—of Henry Ford's treatment of his own son, his employees, and minorities are certainly worth exploring.

To imply that these heroic yet culpable human beings are not worthy of our study is the antithesis of what education should be. Unfortunately, this happened in 1996 in Richmond Hill, Georgia, when a local librarian told a school board member's daughter precisely this,[ii] even though Henry Ford literally gave Richmond Hill its name through his many beneficial actions there. (See Chapter 7.) The life of Henry Ford generated such storm-tossed waves that their last wake still resounds upon the shore.

History is the record of those who take the time to write it down or to preserve the artifacts, homes, and monuments that can speak of their deeds long after they are gone. Henry Ford's historic legacy in Richmond Hill speaks for itself today to those who take the time to ferret it out, or to obtain permission to see it as I was so fortunate to do. Henry Ford is labeled with one of the most famous misunderstood quotes of all recorded time: "History is bunk!" That was the media bite that still resounds, but what Ford meant and detailed was that history is meaningless when only mouthed as dates and battles, but instead must be connected with action that addresses the needs of the people today.

H.G. Cooper was the African American Henry Ford personally selected among seven finalists chosen to be the principal of his newly built George Washington Carver Elementary School, which set a new standard for the education of black Americans in Georgia, or, for that matter, the nation. When asked if Ford treated the African American community as well as the white, Cooper responded with a twinkle in his eye, "Sometimes a little better." Once Cooper refused to shake Mr. Ford's proffered hand because his hands were dirty from digging up sweet potatoes. Ford stooped down and rubbed some dirt together and then offered his hand again. Ford, the kinesthetic learner and doer, never much with words, spoke volumes in that simple act. Cooper, now a distinguished funeral home director in Darien, Georgia, found such acts repeated throughout his nine years of working for Ford from 1937 to 1946.

Ford used to tell Cooper that tough times make you stronger. Cooper especially remembered these words that helped him chart a successful and respected life: "Don't expect anybody to give you anything. You can do two times as much anyway if you do it for yourself. What I wish is a new attitude free from greed, and the idea that any permanent good can come from overreaching others, and above all, to live your life with the expectancy of change."[iii]

Henry Ford's great vision for Richmond Hill, Georgia, as well as this nation, is exemplified by his acts of historic restoration and development, not only in Georgia but elsewhere as well. In Massachusetts, he restored and built a series of buildings centered around the Wayside Inn of Longfellow fame, one of the oldest inns in America. In his hometown of Dearborn, Michigan, he created the largest indoor/outdoor museum complex in the world. The truth is that each of these communities can create a better home for themselves and their children with such vision. By using the historic landmarks Ford saved and built as anchors to our past, the storms of change that grow ever more violent in our respective communities can be weathered. "Future shock"

is everywhere. Ford saw it coming decades before the book of the same title was written. He saw it coming because he in great part made it possible when he perfected the moving assembly line mass manufacturing methods that allowed for a flood of affluence and goods.

"Many men do not seem to know that yesterday is past. They wake up this morning with last year's ideas,"[iv] is another Ford quote that can be easily misunderstood similar to his "History is bunk!" statement. As shown by his actions in Richmond Hill in Georgia, the Wayside Inn of Massachusetts, and his hometown of Dearborn, Ford was neither fixed in the past nor overly driven toward the future. He saw the importance of both, and he used the best of the past to set a standard of excellence and beauty for what must be added or completed today.

Richmond Hill, Georgia; Dearborn, Michigan; South Sudbury, Massachusetts; our nation and our world—all are at the turning point. Change is everywhere. The past—not only of Henry Ford but of those generations before him—resides and abounds in these towns and many others. As Ford suggested, it would indeed be a crime to let greed overreach the needs of present and future generations. It would be a missed opportunity to anchor our present lives to it, not only as we struggle with the seas of change but also as we act on behalf of our children to enrich and enliven the legacy that Ford left. By pushing the envelope of industrial, agricultural, and historic preservation technology, and then promoting and (for the most part) practicing fair treatment and prosperity for all, Ford left a legacy not only to be proud of, but upon which to build.

Ford lived his life similar to the tide—forward thinking, backward thinking, the best of old, the best of new, sometimes high, and sometimes low. Ford never forgot. He was as proud as any, but he tried and often succeeded in living a humble servant life in response to another, much more powerful, perfect orbit: God. It is not politically correct to say that God rules your life these days, but Ford is quoted in a chapel program by Lester Twork as saying, "During the first World War, Woodrow Wilson and I took a pledge together to read a chapter of the Bible every day. I have kept my pledge, and I understand that he did until his death."[v] For many years, Twork was a guide at Ford's Dearborn estate and once was Ford's chemistry teacher at Camp Legion. It was here that Ford gave education, nondenominational chapel services, and work opportunities to wounded and "shell-shocked" veterans during the years of World War II.

In the Old Testament of the Bible, Ford read the stories of many great heroes of Israel, Abraham, David, and Solomon, and in the New Testament of Peter, Paul, and Christ. His favorite passage was "Faith is the substance of things hoped for, the evidence of things not seen." This verse of scripture is used by Ford to close his autobiography, *My Life and Work* (1922). Jim Newton of Ft. Myers, Florida, both my friend and a friend of Ford, also quoted this verse as being Ford's favorite. Jim was in his early nineties when he shared in writing and orally with me his firsthand perspectives of Ford's spiritual beliefs. After the death of his only son Edsel, Henry Ford had a lot of soul-searching to do. His hope in the end is emblazoned on his tomb—a Christian cross. The auto-king is dead, but his dreams remain alive in dozens of historic sites and factories that were built for the great multitude, including generations yet unborn.

Henry's wife Clara was never enthusiastic about the Richmond Hill grand social experiment, one reason being that she did not like the clouds of sand gnats which could engulf people there. However, she did not dissuade Henry from doing what he felt compelled to do. She remained ever the believer, as the one biography in her honor is titled, and she joined in the effort.

Both Fords were doers. Perhaps this is the greatest lesson a dead billionaire can teach us today. H.G. Cooper recalls riding in the car with Clara when they came upon a group of black laborers working hard in the sun, while the white foreman stood there and gave instructions. Cooper, an African American raised in the South, soon was asked to tell the foreman that he should his give instructions by grabbing a shovel himself.[vi] Henry and Clara could have retired to Florida, Hawaii, or anywhere, spending their latter years in reclusion. Instead, they found joy in giving and doing, through restoration and building. This, if you read the Bible—whether the Old or New Testament, Proverbs, or St. Paul—is the path to joy. Run the race of life to its end according to the pull of another orbit, as the moon pulls the tide upward and downward, forward and backward, high and low. Like life.

Notes to the Reader

This interpretive biography uses oral history, pictures, and songs written to strengthen the insights that are shared. Each can be used to read or even "sing" this book. Ballads were among the first forms of biography. Thus, it is appropriate to include both historic and contemporary ballads to tell the story of Henry Ford. Those insights are based on 16 years of research and literally working in and interpreting the landmarks Ford left as his legacy. In many instances, there were too many sources to footnote every fact. Thus, in some ways, this is a consensus biography taken from those who lived both in Ford's shadow and apart.

AS THE CENTURY TURNS

Music & lyrics by Donn P. Werling

As the cen-tu-ry turns there are les-sons to learn of peo-ple who lived and gave___ to us_____ a le- ga- cy of a cen- tu- ry that trans- formed the world all___ a- round_____. 1. So sing of the men and wo- men who lived; think on their trials, the joy their gifts give, the strug-gles for free- dom from ty- rants and toil, the gifts and the pro- blems of a world run on oil. As the

2. With his feet in the past, he built foundations that last;
   Henry Ford brought a flood of consumer goods.
   He paid people well, but sometimes his deed fell;
   He made mistakes like you, like me.

3. Martha Berry of Rome was a saint you will see
   Who gained some of Ford's millions and more.
   Like Ford she built well, but was never a "swell",
   And worked as a servant of her Lord Jesus Christ.

4. Harvey Firestone of tire making fame
   Launched the career of a Jim Newton by name
   Who knew all the men — his uncommon friends —
   And helped launch a promotion of friendship for all.

5. Wild goose Jack loved Canada's out back
   But made his home a refuge for gesse.
   His clear eye could see the century's need
   To conserve all the birds, the geese, the trees.

6. Lindbergh the ace of both peace and war
   Behind German lines, what he saw he abhorred.
   He pleaded for time to match them, to win,
   And suffered much pain although much adored.

CHAPTER ONE

CORNERSTONES

On the river side of the powerhouse of Fair Lane, Henry Ford's 1,200-acre Dearborn estate, is a large stone curved staircase leading down to where Thomas Edison laid the cornerstone of record for the structure. The cornerstone for the residence was left unmarked to fall into obscurity. Also, it is illustrative to note that Fair Lane does not conform to the north-south, east-west coordinates of the Northwest Territorial Act and of surveyors; rather, it follows the bluff of the Rouge River. Therefore, its directions are dictated by

1914	$5 a day wage
	First met Jack Miner
1914–1918	*World War I*
1915	Fair Lane completed
	Bought the bungalow in the Upper Peninsula
1916	Bought home in Ft. Myers
1917	Fordson tractor
	Birth of Henry Ford II, the first of four grandchildren
1918	Migratory Bird Treaty with Canada
1918–1924	"Four Vagabonds" camping trips
1919	Ford sole owner of Ford Motor Company
1919–1927	X engine (The engine/car that never was)
1921	First met Martha Berry
1922	Lincoln Motor Company purchased
1924	Built first diesel freighters on the Great Lakes
1925	Admitted to Huron Mt. Club
	Began acquiring Georgia land
1926	Ford Tri-motor
1927	Model A introduced; Model T discontinued

nature, and terms such as "riverside" and "path of the setting sun in summer" are descriptors that were used both historically and today as well. The large stones of the curved staircase architecturally repeat for Henry Ford the admonition that we are to go down to see not only the cornerstone of his powerhouse, but to see who was the cornerstone of his success.

On October 28, 1914, Thomas Alva Edison laid the cornerstone at Henry Ford's final home, Fair Lane, at the base of the powerhouse, overlooking the river of Ford's youth and old age. Henry Ford was 51 years old at the time of the cornerstone laying. His goal was to live to be 100 years old, but his life lasted only an active 83 years.

Ford probably reflected that it was Thomas Edison's encouragement of his gasoline-propelled automobile, when most thought electric battery propulsion was the wave of the future, that was a cornerstone in helping Ford move ahead despite the "doubting Thomases." Coming from the electrical wizard himself, not his words as much as his slap on the table—a "Yes! Go do it, young man!" command to seize the moment—made Ford's vision for the future suddenly seem within his grasp. The rest is history.

Henry Ford's boyhood idol, Thomas Edison, eventually became his manhood friend, but perhaps Ford wondered if Edison accepted his invitation to lay the cornerstone of the powerhouse while thinking of a Ford market for Edison's new electric battery. Ford must have regretted that the battery did not have the power to work in his experimental electric car. It was to have been named the Edison-Ford. Edison's salesman tried to sell Ford an order for 100,000 batteries before Ford had even test run them in a car! However, to Ford's way of thinking, that did not matter. Edison's presence at the laying of the cornerstone sufficed. Edison's presence was important not only for this ceremonial moment, but for the future as well. The large stones of the outdoor curved staircase leading down from the powerhouse then and now tell the world for generations to come to see who was the cornerstone of Ford's success. Edison gave Ford not only words, but also a slap on the table, signaling both applause and encouragement—applause for Ford's idea that the gasoline car would propel the world into the auto age, and encouragement to not hesitate, to not doubt, but instead to roll up his sleeves and embrace the struggle that the realization of an idea entails. Ford admired Edison as much for his gritty earthiness as for his technical achievements. Genius, Ford must have realized, is truly as Edison had said: "One percent inspiration and ninety-nine percent perspiration."

Thus started, the powerhouse provided the fires for the origins of many ideas. Ford wanted to hone these ideas into service for a world that needed a Model T of the soil as much as it needed a Model T car—a world that needed a prototype which could apply the benefits of hydroelectricity and technology to agriculture on a scale that did not overwhelm nature, but worked with

nature as Emerson wrote. The drudgery, irascibility, and dung of the horse age seemed doomed to fall. The new birth of freedom for this century and beyond had begun, much as it did for the founding fathers and Abraham Lincoln.

The Fair Lane powerhouse, circa 1920. An eight-foot dam on the Rouge River slightly upstream powered twin 55-kilowatt generators. The cornerstone was laid by Thomas Alva Edison on October 28, 1914, and remains in place today. It lies at the base of a spiral of stone stairs (slightly to the right of the large tree in the center of the photograph). Henry Ford's Experimental Room was the top floor of the powerhouse, with the garage opposite the river and the greenhouses to the right. Ford was embarrassed at the size of the main residence; however, the powerhouse—with its clean, utilitarian lines and aura of purposefulness—was his pride and joy. (Photograph from the Collections of Henry Ford Museum & Greenfield Village)

The powerhouse, laboratory, and garage complex for which Edison set the cornerstone still defies conventional description. The wooden trellis across the front of the garage is adorned with 100 orange trumpets from the trumpet vine, calling to hummingbirds with an offer of food and refreshment, as well as to cars, tractors, and trucks. The generator room has both state-of-the-art electrical generators and the vintage Armington and Sims steam-powered generator, which Edison used to bring electricity to the world and Ford, who had been the chief engineer for the local electrical utility, to Detroit. There Ford placed twin birds upon a branch of peace in the ceiling ventilator grill covers. To Henry Ford, peace meant peace with nature and peace with technology, created from the power of the river—the simple, peaceful power of the river in which Ford swam as a youth, and the Rouge River of his home for 30 years.

Today, the roar of the river behind the cornerstone still provides a sense of power and delight in its sunlit cascade. The steppingstones lead across the top of the dam to the other bank, to Ford's old friends and relatives, whose homes remain upon the other shore. Turning back, we can view the twin castles of Fair Lane. One is a castle with its battlefront walls, parapet, and tower, resembling a storybook picture from another century. The other is the powerhouse, with its modern lines, wooden overhangs, and the spirit of the century of Henry Ford's life. It is the herald of all things new, while cloaked in nature's sparkling garments and shoes. Water glistens before it and through it, trees soar, birds sing of rapprochement with nature and freedom that has given us the peaceful beauty of the country while providing all the conveniences of the city. That is the cornerstone that Thomas Edison, the greatest of all inventors, laid on that important day in October 1914. The slap of Edison's mortar, similar to the slap of his encouraging hand, solidified and remained for decades more, supporting Ford's powerhouse and laboratories in which Ford and his men worked to both invent the future and preserve the past.

This powerhouse, beginning at the base far beneath the earth, where venturi discharge accelerators double the height of this eight-foot dam through the "magic" of innovative engineering, has its foundation built on the future. Its cornerstone was laid in the spirit of friendship, with selfless encouragement to the next generation. It is indeed a powerhouse of which to be proud, as much for what it did in its first century as for how it will be viewed 1,000 years from now. Henry Ford always told Edsel that if one built well, what was built would always find a future. As the Englishman John Ruskin wrote in *The Builders*[1-1], it is in the attention and wrestling with wrought substance that we build "...not for present delight nor for present use alone...[but] that men will say as they look upon the labor and wrought substance of them, 'See this our fathers did for us.' "

The 1914 Ford experimental electric car. Having been encouraged by Thomas Edison in 1895 to pursue the gasoline-powered automobile, Ford hoped to return the compliment using Edison's new batteries. However, they did not meet specifications, and Ford dropped the project. Business was business, and the five charging ports for electric cars in Ford's new garage went largely unused except for Clara's Detroit Electric. (Photograph from the Collections of Henry Ford Museum & Greenfield Village)

Both Henry and Clara selected the site for their dream home at the bend of the Rouge River, with vistas upstream and downstream. The water's roar soothed away fears, and the lines of hydraulic and ground energy that flow there both lighted and lifted life's path to a wider horizon. The energy of this place was and remains a force for good.

The Ford boathouse, circa 1923. The Rouge River was a ribbon of pleasure and profit for the Fords. It linked Henry Ford's past to his estate at Fair Lane, his museum and historical village, and the Rouge factory complex. All three are now National Historic Landmarks in the Rouge Corridor of the Automobile National Heritage Area established by Congress with the President's signature in November, 1998. (Photograph from the Collections of Henry Ford Museum & Greenfield Village)

The powerhouse, laboratory, garage, furniture restoration room, and Edison memorial complex at Fair Lane, Henry Ford's 1,200-acre estate, defies any one descriptor. To refer to the structure as only a power-house conjures up much too simplistic a vision. The six-level beehive of innovation and modernity, which lies south of the residence and is connected by a 300-foot tunnel, rises modestly yet strongly from a bank carved into the bluff of the Rouge River.

A consulting engineer from the University of Michigan, seeing that the river offered only an eight-foot head of water, said the river was inadequate to make a hydroelectric installation economical or practical. Most

would have taken his advice and foregone the building of a dam and hydropower on the site. However, Ford sought further advice and turned to Mark A. Replogle of waterpower-rich New England. Replogle provided what became the ultimate solution—venturi discharge accelerators. Three headraces were built, with the center one doing nothing other than creating a venturi by adding water to the point of discharge. This created a draft effect that literally pulled the water through the turbines. Once installed, measurements were taken, and it was discovered that by harnessing the venturi effect, an eight-foot-high dam functioned the same as one twice its size. This triumph was trumpeted in an early publication of The American Society for Mechanical Engineers in December 1915. Taking a quote from Henry Ford's *My Life and My Work*, "Everything was made possible,"[1-2] even though it had been deemed by a college man as impossible. Ford was always proud of his powerhouses and made display objects of them on many occasions. The power that spawned production was utmost, and he wanted to make it foremost in the minds of his guests and visitors as well.

Ford's Fair Lane powerhouse chimney is impressive, but perhaps the most elegant smokestack in the world a half-mile distant co-stars in the nighttime view of Dearborn, along with Ford's reproduction of the Independence Hall tower. For guests at Ford's Dearborn Inn, the two stand like light-houses, illuminating Ford's life amid an otherwise pedestrian nightscape. Albert Kahn designed the smokestack as part of the Elm Street Power Station for the 1920s state-of-the-art engineering complex, which remains in use today. When built, it was the tallest suspended masonry smokestack structure in the world. This feat of engineering seems to defy gravity and continues to greet Ford engineers today as Ford Motor Company celebrates the centennial of its founding, a milestone few corporations survive to face. Today, the company is still intact, the second-largest automaker in the world. Professor David Lewis of the University of Michigan School of Business

Henry Ford, shown here in his fifties, is standing beside the Rouge River of his destiny. (Photograph from the Collections of Henry Ford Museum & Greenfield Village)

said in his biography of Henry Ford that the company itself is Ford's greatest monument. It is testimony to its founder, his heirs, and the resiliency of the Great Lakes region that spawned this colossus.

In many ways, Henry Ford's outlook was shaped in the pre-Titanic era when all things did seem possible. So too it is at Fair Lane, Ford's home for thirty-one years. The tallest, the boldest, and by far the strongest architectural element is not the half-castle tower of the residence; rather, it is the massive and beautiful monolithic chimney that rises to a concrete-capped summit above the topmost roof of the powerhouse. The entire Estate was designed with much of the spirit of the Prairie School, if not completely in the Prairie style. This style is captured by the large, striking chimney of the powerhouse combined with the original site location carved into the river bluff, giving the overall appearance of a structure much smaller than six levels yet more than eighty feet high and the equivalent of an eight-story building. The chimney is located in the center of the building, as Ford felt all domes-

tic chimneys should be positioned. This complex was to be as much his home as the main residence one hundred yards upstream. It was available at all hours of the day and night, with the prime view and restful sound of the waterfall associated with his workspace, not the residence.

The powerhouse indeed became a force for good, as Ford had hoped when he watched Edison lay its cornerstone. Its greatest success was that the complex itself became a prototype for his Village Industries program, which many have cited as the first example of the decentralization, or mass movement, of industry to greener fields. Although this movement left old industrial land to languish while green fields became factory sites, it is also true that one of Ford's goals, admired and recommended by Frank Lloyd Wright, has been realized. People have been brought closer to nature.

Having built the world's largest concentration of industry at that time, both Ford and his wife Clara began to have second thoughts about the impact on quality of life that the migration from farm to factory caused in the early twentieth century. Such concern motivated Clara to work with the Woman's National Farm and Garden Clubs in Detroit and to serve as the national president for two terms in the 1920s. Gardening was not only a means by which a woman could help support her family—it was a way of staying in touch with the good earth. Henry Ford likewise promoted gardening. The memories of garden plots provided by Ford during the hard times of the 1930s, as well as the war years, are ones that hundreds recall, not as "plantation" type memories, but as sincere attempts by Ford to enable a person to put food on the table, rather than taking handouts, which Ford abhorred.

To Henry Ford, those programs were merely bandages. His move to the countryside of Dearborn was a step in his vision of providing a means for rural people to remain on the land on a larger scale. By returning to the farming community in which he was raised, Ford's

Fair Lane was in essence the prototype for more than two dozen village industries, with its self-sufficient power source and its niche role in Ford's sprawling corporation. Having created along the Rouge River one of the largest industrial complexes in world history, Ford became a pioneer in decentralization, leading the way to green fields of his past for the betterment of the future of his workers and society. The thrust of bringing power and factory work to the country became a national and international model. (Photograph from the Collections of Henry Ford Museum & Greenfield Village)

own Estate played the role of prototype for the more than 20 water-powered village industries that soon followed. His famous quote, "With one foot on the land and one foot in industry, America is safe,"[1-3] provides insight into Ford's ultimate goals.

Ford's Village Industries program had the following basic ingredients: an independent source of power, usually water but occasionally wood; a rural setting; a mission of supplying one or more components or sub-assembly products for the company; and a limited size of no more than a few hundred workers.

The Fair Lane powerhouse complex meets all of these criteria. It was the first of more than 20 hydropower plants built by Ford. Together with the twin boilers for heat, which first were wood fired and later coke fired, Fair Lane was self-sufficient in theory, if not completely in practice. In 1915, its Dearborn setting was distinctly rural. The mission was to provide the corporate chief executive officer a refuge whereby he could maintain his links to the restorative powers of nature, yet allow for him and his small staff of engineers, watchmakers, and furniture restorers to produce ideas or goods. Production of the latter was centered on the work of Ed Eisel, who restored furniture on the second level of the powerhouse for more than twenty-five years. It was here, with perhaps the best view of the waterscape, that beat-up antiques were brought, completely rebuilt, and then shipped to various locations of Ford's restorations. Henry Ford was as much of a pioneer in historic preservation as he was in the field of automobiles or tractors.

Ford took communion with nature far beyond the simple act of establishing factories in the country. Not only did he contract the noted Prairie School landscape architect, Jens Jensen, to idealize the natural world of the residence, but he also had Jensen do the same at the powerhouse of Fair Lane. Jensen, and after he retired, his son-in-law Marshall Johnson, were hired at many of the village industry sites to create similar bucolic settings, which still exist today.

At Fair Lane, oral history indicates Ford went one more step. W.G. Avery, a driver for Ford from 1918 to 1920,[1-4] recalled various occasions on which he was asked to drive Mr. Ford's Model T back to the Estate so Ford could walk home from his factory as the farmers did from their fields. On another occasion, when the naturalist John Burroughs was tired of touring Henry Ford's factory, Ford had Avery take Burroughs back to Fair Lane via the nature trail, which included a log bridge across the Rouge River. This may have been downstream from the dam, because a steppingstone walkway currently exists across the top of the dam and was enjoyed by Ford and other family members. Despite having automobiles of any size and make at his command, Ford chose to ride his bicycle daily and to walk in the woods. He also encouraged others to bike and skate by always having a rack of bicycles in the garage and skates of any size in the ice skating house by the pond at the end of the meadow.

W.G. Avery began his career with Ford Motor Company, with daily trips to Henry Ford's garage. Some of Avery's other memories offer insight into the early mission of the Fair Lane powerhouse complex. When Avery drove the Model T back to the Estate garage, he often found a variety of cars in various states of assembly and disassembly. Certainly the garage was not designed with automobile research in mind. Oral histories say for want of an overhead hoist, the mechanics used an old black locust tree with an overhanging branch to lift engine blocks from vehicles. The locust tree was thick and strong, dating back to the nineteenth century when the land was owned and farmed by the Black family.

The reason Ford's Estate garage was being put to such intense corporate use perhaps stems from the swirl of events occurring as Ford struggled to capture more complete control of his destiny. The Dodge brothers and other stockholders were both Ford's competitors and partners. Therefore, to protect any new developments to which the Dodges and others could legitimately lay claim if they were produced in Ford Motor Company factories, the evidence indicates that Henry Ford developed them at his privately owned Fair Lane estate. During the time that Ford negotiated the Dodges' buyout, the Fordson tractor came on line as part of a completely separate Henry Ford and Son owned company.

The powerhouse complex, when viewed from the perspective of its entire history, has a curious mix of characteristics, reflecting the thinking and rethinking of a person who over time experienced exhilaration, frustration, and disappointment with his own ideas. The hydropower plant worked almost perfectly until the week Henry Ford died, after the floods rendered it useless. It worked so well that, after maintaining for a decade but never using his back-up battery system, Ford removed the batteries, leaving only the oak shelves in case they were called into service in the future. The Experimental Room on the top floor explored everything from brewing nonalcoholic beer to growing plants in aluminum pots, the latter because a worker claimed he discovered the electrical secret of plants and that they grew faster in aluminum. The famous plant breeder, Luther Burbank, replicated the experiment in California until Thomas Edison debunked the "plant" electrician with a terse letter.

Ford's attempts to develop the successor to the Model T at the Estate met with even less success. This X engine initially was designed at Fair Lane, first by Allen Horton and later redesigned by Eugene Farkas.[1-5] Ford provided the specifications: an X arrangement of pistons and air-cooled, which Farkas later changed to water-cooled.[1-6] All promised to fulfill Ford's dream of a compact, powerful, and light but strong engine that would package into an X-car as revolutionary as the Model T.

Numerous prototypes were made, all with the same result. Harold Hicks put it mildly, "The lubrication wasn't positive enough." Ford's most important criteria—durability—was unattainable. Consequently, Ford was forced into a crash program to build the Model A. Although Henry Ford had ordered Horton to build the successor to the Model T in 1920, the suggestions of Edsel Ford and his brother-in law Ernest Kanzler to move to a different engine for the Model A had been rejected by Henry without consideration.

In an eight-page letter to Henry Ford dated January 26, 1926,[1-7] Kanzler [the archival copy of the letter is unsigned but is presumed to be Kanzler's letter] systematically and sometimes delicately points out the loss of market share in 1924 and 1925 as Model T sales slipped to

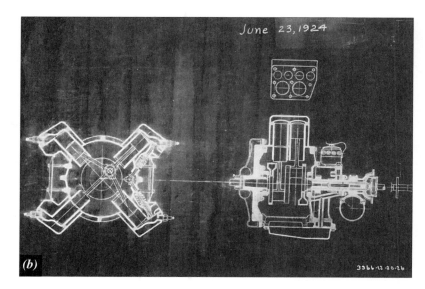

Eugene Farkas worked for Ford on the top floor of Fair Lane's powerhouse Experimental Room, designing the replacement engine that would top the T engine with an X engine. Despite almost a decade of development, the radical design proved a blind alley for automotive applications. However, perhaps it helped lay the groundwork for Ford's V-8 engine, which was the engineering leap forward that Ford had sought to succeed the triumph of the Model T. (a) Eugene Farkas. (b) The design of the X engine. (c) Pistons of the X engine. (d) The water-cooled X engine designed by Farkas. (Photographs from the Collections of Henry Ford Museum & Greenfield Village)

the growing popularity of V-6 powered cars. Kanzler applauds Ford and the X engine with all of it promises, but [in the original letter, the word "but" is fully capitalized] he states:

> Those of us who have been privileged to follow the X [engine] development look into the future and hope for great things, BUT, and this is what worries me, I feel that there should also be other development in process on a power unit along conventional lines so that we would have if necessary a power unit to maintain our position in the automobile field until the X motor is perfected— something that will serve until you will have been given a fair chance to produce the X motors to their final stage of development so that when once adopted they will lead all others for another twenty years like the Model T.

Kanzler continues in his letter to support with facts and figures that the buying public is voting with their pocketbooks for the V-6 engine. That assertion by Kanzler may have been his undoing at Ford, although his letter is well laced with deserved and even undeserved accolades given to Henry Ford, such as:

> …we would sweep all before us with your revolutionary X power plant substituted when its perfection has been achieved.

In spite of the advice of Kanzler and others such as Edsel Ford, Henry Ford was persistent to a fault in regard to keeping the X engine project alive. Thus, he acquired a Model T image of stagnation and of being wedded to his aging triumph, when he simply was reaching too far into the future of engineering and attempting what was thought impossible. Later, Henry Ford did accomplish what seemed impossible: the development of the V-8 engine, cast in a single block. Still being pieced together is what may have been Ford's even grander plan the X engine. He experimented for eight years with the X engine in a racing boat and in cars. In 1925, an X engine drawing for an air-cooled 200 h.p. X engine was found. Correlated with a note in Harold Hicks' oral history that around the same time Billy Mitchell of Army Air Force fame stopped by to review their plans, one is moved to wonder if Ford's dream for the universal car had expanded to the economies of

scale that a universal engine would produce. Perhaps in one bold stroke Ford hoped not only to maintain supremacy on land but to rule the waters and the air as well. Such a vision indeed would have been hard to let go, and oral histories suggest that the potential of the X engine remained with Henry Ford until his death.

The laboratory equipment of the top-level Experimental Room of the powerhouse was largely removed in 1925 when Ford cleared it to make a dancing practice room. The engineering building on the twin ponds had been open for some time with expanded research facilities. All that Ford allowed to remain was the subdivided room with drafting tables for his engineers to work on special projects, which centered on tractors. When Fair Lane was built, the Fordson tractor was in its final development. Thus, the powerhouse had come full circle. It continued to provide a refuge for watchmaking, tinkering, and, in the afternoons, dancing. Not even the boiler operators were safe from Ford's messianic zeal when it came to dancing. John McIntyre, known as Scotty,[1-8] was even enlisted to demonstrate the Schottische to the tunes of Ford's live orchestra. The orchestra enjoyed using the top floor of the powerhouse at Fair Lane to practice for the big dances that moved to the engineering building and later to Lovett Hall, now the education building between the museum and Greenfield Village.

Fair Lane's powerhouse/Experimental Room did not become a Henry Ford version of the Edison invention factory, which he may have partially intended. Ford was not as much an inventor as he was a synergizer. In response to a media query as to how he accomplished so much, Ford once said that he never really did anything except go around and light fires under everyone. The powerhouse began with Edison laying the cornerstone. It did not end with any of the failures or successes that occurred within its walls. The wave of decentralization of industry to rural areas, sweeping across the country and to many foreign lands, replicated Ford's vision. It is proof of the power of his idea. It is true that his grandson, Henry Ford II, closed many of the relatively small village industries, the last and oldest being Northville (established in 1919 and closed in 1992). However, the many outlying new Ford plants built during Henry Ford II's presidency of Ford Motor Company have a similar overlay pattern, which brought work out to the green fields of exurbia for farmer and suburbanite. How much Ford's development began or accelerated this trend can be argued, but Ford's intent seemed clear. His goal was no less than a recreation of the Jeffersonian ideal. Emerson and Ford's birds of peace, under the two ventilator stacks of the generator room and above his state-of-the-art hydroelectric plant, clearly indicate their belief that technology and nature can work together for good. Furthermore, given the option, we should work in and with nature's bounty. As Ford said, "With one foot on the land and one foot in industry, America is safe."[1-9]

CORNERSTONES

Music & Lyrics by Donn P. Werling

There are stones to build and stones to throw:

One is large, one needs____ to grow. For the cor- ner

stones of hu - man life Are built on love sur -

mount - ing strife____ The wi- zard of light, the

wi- zard of sound: Tom Ed- i -son's name 'round the world__ re -

sounds. And when young Ford showed him his plans He

said go a- head, that's it young man!

Copyright 1997 Donn P. Werling

CHAPTER TWO

FAIR LANE'S GARAGE

In 1993, when the University of Michigan–Dearborn constructed the long-awaited grounds maintenance structure, Fair Lane's garage was freed for the first time since the University of Michigan had received Fair Lane as a gift. The estate was given to the university by Ford Motor Company in 1956, seven years after the death of Clara Ford at Henry Ford Hospital. The rallying cry became the idea that if anyone's garage should be restored, it should be Henry's. Now, thanks to the leadership of Edsel B. Ford II and the generosity of Ford family members and dealers from across the country and of Ford Motor Company itself, the garage at Fair Lane has been restored. Research into the structure and the cars once housed there was fascinating because company and personal history are intertwined there as nowhere else at the Estate.

Photographs show that the garage once was both an estate garage and a showplace museum for Ford's early vehicles, such as the quadricycle that Ford tracked down and partially restored. Changes, showing more

1918–1924	"Four Vagabonds" camping trips
1919	Ford sole owner of Ford Motor Company
1919–1927	X engine (The engine/car that never was)
1921	First met Martha Berry
1922	Lincoln Motor Company purchased
1924	Built first diesel freighters on the Great Lakes
1925	Admitted to Huron Mt. Club
	Began acquiring Georgia land
1926	Ford Tri-motor
1927	Model A introduced; Model T discontinued

openly the working mechanisms of the car, were made during the Selden patent suit and left on display. (Selden had claimed the patent without ever building his car.) In this famous lawsuit, Ford's triumph over the East Coast Association of Licensed Automobile Manufacturing on the entire concept of the automobile had made Ford a champion of the little guy. Although his company had initially joined the Selden trust, Ford came to balk at the per-car charge of the East Coast licensers, who dealt only with paper and never steel or rubber, similar to the financiers Ford detested. Having the quadricycle in the garage of the Ford estate was not simply the preservation of a memory; it was a compass pointing to the direction Ford charted for himself and his company.

Ford would bow to no one—except to Clara, of course, who liked Cadillacs. Automotive historian Randy Mason suggested that Clara's Cadillacs may have reminded Henry of his roots because Henry had helped found that company before establishing Ford Motor Company in 1903. Regardless, Ford bought the Lincoln Motor Company in 1922, perhaps for two reasons: (1) Clara could have a Ford product, and (2) Edsel could build upon it, ultimately designing one of the first cars (the 1939 Lincoln Continental) to be displayed in the Museum of Modern Art in New York.

Over the years, various numbers have been cited as to how many cars were held in the garage in Ford's heyday. Written records are inconsistent, but estimates range from seven to seventeen. The latter number is possible, particularly when calculating spatial requirements for Model T cars and a quadricycle. However, jamming that many cars into the 2,000 square feet of Ford's personal garage probably would have occurred only under extraordinary circumstances.

When W.G. Avery worked at the garage for Henry Ford circa 1918 to 1919, it was a time of extraordinary circumstances. In the late 1980s, near the end of his long life, Mr. Avery unexpectedly stopped at Fair Lane in his chauffeur-driven Cadillac. During his visit, he spoke with Bruno Gluski, a University of Michigan–Dearborn engineer. Gluski recognized that Mr. Avery was a historical gold mine, and he also realized that I, as Director of the Estate, should be summoned. Following his visit to Fair Lane, Avery donated a four-figure check to the Estate.

As a young man getting his start, Avery had worked for Ford at the old tractor plant, where the Henry Ford Museum now stands. The tractor plant was less than a mile "as the crow flies" from Ford's Fair Lane. Avery distinctly remembered Mr. Ford eschewing his car to walk home through the woods and across the river on a log pontoon bridge. It had been the first time anyone at Fair Lane had ever heard of this bridge, but there were a few people still alive with firsthand memories of that era.

The exterior view of the Fair Lane garage. The garage housed many vehicles over the years, including experimental tractors and tear downs of cars manufactured by competitors, a Cadillac for Clara Ford until Henry Ford bought the Lincoln Motor Company, and, of course, a Model T, a Model A, and Ford's last car powered by the revolutionary V-8 engine. (Photograph from the Collections of Henry Ford Museum & Greenfield Village)

dam. What were unusual were the activities that Avery remembers as occurring in the garage when he returned Henry Ford's Model T one particular evening.

The garage at Fair Lane there held more than Ford cars and more than Edsel's Marmon, which was a Jaguar-like car of its day. Avery remembers seeing Chevrolets and other cars in various stages of assembly and disassembly. In short, the Fair Lane garage was serving as a corporate research laboratory.

Randy Mason notes that Ford had many other facilities available in Dearborn, leading to the question of why all the cars were jammed in his estate garage rather than elsewhere. Furthermore, the engine blocks of many cars were removed by using a block and tackle tied to a sturdy old black locust tree that had survived from the Black farm landscape of the nineteenth century. (The Black farm had occupied the site that became the Fair Lane estate.) The estate garage had not been built with heavy maintenance or experimentation in mind. Henry Ford now was using his own garage for his quest to wrench total control of the company for his family. Any work done in a Ford Motor Company garage would be in full view of the competitors Henry wanted to buy out, such as the stockholding Dodge brothers. Hoped-for innovations such as the X engine, or breakthroughs discovered

Because Henry Ford's car would remain at work on those days when he chose to walk home, Avery would drive Ford's Model T back to the garage at Fair Lane. The image of Henry Ford dancing across a log bridge is not remarkable because he, his nieces, and his guests were known to dance along a stepping-stone bridge across the top of the Ford by Ford while examining the vehicles of the competition, would be accessible to them if not done covertly, therefore increasing the value of the stock Ford wished to depress and then buy. Henry and Clara Ford had the garage and powerhouse built one hundred yards from the residence to ensure tranquility in the residence. However, in the end, everything worked together to create the desired effect—if you were a Ford, that is. During this time, Henry and Clara Ford left their son Edsel in charge as the new president and went to see the sights out West, effectively severing communication with other stockholders.

Today, the garage stands restored, although not to its short role as Ford's secret corporate research headquarters held during perhaps the coup of his lifetime. It is a historical echo that Ford dealers around the country responded so generously to restore. Henry Ford's ploys aimed at lowering the price of Ford Motor Company stock worked in those waning years before the Roaring Twenties began. Henry would no longer have to deal with stockholders who did not share his great vision for the Rouge River and other projects if he could finance the buy-out, which was still at a staggering price. Rather than turn to Wall Street and financiers, Henry turned to an innovative strategy: If you don't want to deal with a few big banks or financiers, then turn to many small banks. Henry's financial ties to those banks were already in place—his seven thousand car dealers. The power and credit-worthiness of his dealers could be used to win this battle, wresting control and financial independence as few in history have done.

Thomas Alva Edison had laid the cornerstone at the powerhouse, garage, and laboratory complex of Fair Lane. Today's guests will see a variety of Ford vehicles there. The one non-Ford vehicle is not Clara's Cadillac; rather, it is a Detroit Electric similar to the one Clara drove. Ford had hoped to work with Edison to make the electric car for the ages, in the same way he had made the Model T for the ages;

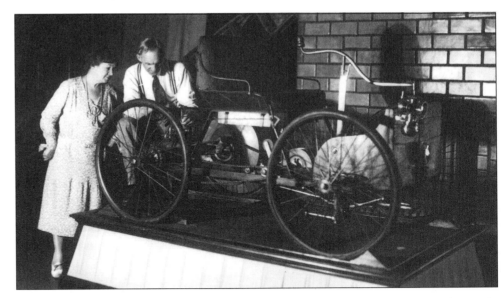

Henry and Clara Ford are shown here in one of the few photographs of them together in the Fair Lane garage. The 3,000-square-foot garage housed antiques such as this 1896 quadricycle and other vehicles such as the Arrow, in which Henry Ford set the world's land speed record in 1904. (Photograph from the Collections of Henry Ford Museum & Greenfield Village)

however, it was not to be. There were five charging ports for electric cars, but probably only one or two were ever used. (Clara's friends also drove electric cars.) Ford cancelled the order for 100,000 of Edison's batteries because an electric car powered by them would not have improved on what Clara already drove.

Too many professors of business ignore the raw business savvy that Henry Ford displayed in his life. He had obvious failures, but his great-grandchildren today and an even newer generation making its way through one of the richest and most successful family-held and then family-controlled corporations of all time, have not forgotten. Most historic estate garages are musty afterthoughts to the main tour. At Fair Lane, the garage is the main event in more ways than one.

Edsel Ford sits in his 1913 Model T roadster. Edsel stored his sporty Marmon at Fair Lane, but he lived less than a year at his parents' new estate before marrying Eleanor Clay in the fall of 1916. (Photograph from the Collections of Henry Ford Museum & Greenfield Village)

Top Floor of the Powerhouse: Ford's Experimental Room

Allen Horton was one of Ford's engineers who was privileged to work in the Experimental Room on the top floor of the powerhouse. His senior partner by 10 years was Harold Hicks, who worked as an associate. Down a half-mile drive past woodland flowers and tall trees,

Horton would take the lower powerhouse drive, park his car, and punch in at the time clock in the gardeners' tool room beneath Clara's range of 100-foot-long greenhouses. Horton then would walk the 50 paces to the lower powerhouse, to the pump room door, and then ascend the 38 steps to Ford's Experimental Room. Today, the room is a cathedral of light, with the tops of trees billowing above the riverscape and accompanied by the spring song of the Jens Jensen-designed cascade. The portion of river water that did not generate electricity did the "work" of inspiring Ford and his most intimate engineering associates. The Experimental Room usually was the first stop in Henry Ford's busy day. Ford, who walked through the tunnel or past Edison's cornerstone to get there, engaged his engineers in conversation on a daily basis when he was in town. Horton, similar to Henry Ford, was self-taught; Hicks had a university education.

Henry Ford gave Horton one of the most critical assignments in Ford Motor Company history—the design of the replacement engine for the Model T. In 1919, Henry Ford conceived the idea for a radical new engine, and the first patent was issued in 1920. Ford had great confidence in Horton. He told Horton of the assignment after hours, and he warned Horton that he would laugh when Ford described the new idea. The Experimental Room was the setting Ford wanted to use to make the impossible happen.

Henry Ford said that he had an idea for a radical rearrangement of cylinders and pistons in an 'X' formation to maximize the power-to-weight ratio. He wanted more power but less weight, with the engine so balanced that you could stand a pencil on it while the engine was running. Ford wanted to top his "T" with an "X." It was easy enough to draw and work with Henry Ford each day when he stopped by the Experimental Room and offered suggestions, but making this engine come to life and remain alive was another challenge. Horton eventually "threw in the towel," and Henry Ford assigned Eugene Farkas to take over the project. Horton felt his reputation as an engineer was at stake. Henry Ford was persistent, and he would wait "until kingdom come" before he brought out anything less.[2-1]

Similar to a part-time cheerleader, critic, and interloper, Henry Ford would enter the Experimental Room brimming with confidence. Failure was not an option. Ford was sure that the X engine would do great things. He remembered seeing such an arrangement years ago on a steam engine. If a mechanic could make such an engine run with steam, Ford was certain they could make the same engine configuration run with gas. He foresaw problems in designing both lubrication and cooling systems with so much power at the core. The patents started coming, and Horton's doubts continued to grow until he resigned. The Experimental Room never made one invention per day, a quota suggested by Edison, but Ford thought the X engine would get things rolling. Furthermore, the Dodge brothers would not know about the engine here in Henry Ford's powerhouse. Ford had said that he wanted to be able to test the wildest ideas without anyone knowing about them. Ford, the master publicist, also wanted to control leaks and to set his own timing. He was confident that the X-engine-powered car would make a bigger splash than the Model T. Sales of the Model T were still rising, but Ford must have believed it was not too soon to reach and grab for his next star.

The allure of the X engine stemmed from a variety of advantages it offered over the Model T engine, whose shake and sideways shimmy were as much a part of the Model T experience as going forward or backward. The X design of the engine arranged the cylinders into a compact balanced mass. Sorenson literally balanced a pencil on a prototype vehicle powered by the hum of an X engine.

Ford liked to take things to the extreme and then pull back to a production model. His old car racing experience as a world land speed record holder probably was of the same mentality that is advertised on television by automakers today. With the X engine, Ford chose in 1921 to make a racing boat the extreme test rather than a car. The only problem was that when the boat was completed, there was not another boat like it to form a racing class. Dubbed "Miss Dearborn," the boat was specified by Henry Ford himself to have 4400 cubic inches of refined power from its twenty-four cylinders using four blocks cast in the X engine design.[2-2] By 1922 or 1923, they had the boat running, or rather "humming," to everyone's satisfaction. It could also set you on your *derriere*, as it did Harold Hicks when the captain laid on the throttle. Hicks designed the boat in tandem with Allen Horton, who started the engine design. It could propel its thirty-three-foot length and nine-foot beam sixty miles an hour, and it did not take long to get up to speed. Tested on a dynamometer, the engine had 1000 horsepower as planned. Henry Ford's son Edsel had streamlined everything, including pop-up headlights and even the tie-up cleats. The X design produced exactly what Henry wanted: power smoother than a well-oiled sewing machine. Scaled down to the power needed to replace the Model T, it would be a compact but power-packed engine. However, a boat would not have the problem of oil fouling the lower plugs as could occur in a car because the plugs in the boat were placed in the vicinity of the exhaust valves to blow away excess oil.

Ford's use of a marine application to test the X design was fostered by Edsel's love of racing boats, among other factors. In a sense, Ford was repeating his own engineering training which had come not in college but in the marine works of Detroit. He had worked there with a master Great Lakes boat buider, Frank Kirby, whose name is inscribed alongside the names of Edison, Carver, and others on the triple E building in Dearborn. This landmark, designed by Albert Kahn, stands by the twin ponds along Oakwood Boulevard next to Ford's other great monument, the Edison Institute (since renamed the Henry Ford Museum).

The test was expensive. Harold Hicks recalled the cost of the X-powered boat in the early 1920s to be $125,000. The beauty of the engine and its power, balance, and smooth running characteristics had all been proven. The Model T production continued to soar but was soon to taper off and plummet, as Chevrolet with its in-line six and others were starting to rise to the sales challenge of the formerly dominant T. Ford knew the X engine had the potential.

Although the boat application had not tested the road conditions that would cause fouling of the lower plugs in a car, it had pointed out the Achilles' heel that Ford, his engineers, and 1920s technology could not solve. With an X engine, much of the heat generated from combustion and friction was not dissipated; rather, it was concentrated in the core. Ford's first X engine was small and air-cooled and, by virtue of its mass, avoided the heat problem. However, when stepped up in size, its bearings failed. The asset of compactness became a liability, or at minimum a design challenge. Although the engine would hum like a sewing machine, the heat soon would take its toll, and the connecting rods would burn out. Henry Ford had designed a special lubrication "splash-type" system, but it had not worked effectively. The crankshafts held up well as they endured much less stress, given the balanced nature of the X design. The challenge Ford set for his engineers was to reduce the engine size and solve the twin problems of plug fouling and lubrication. Unfortunately, they did not meet Henry's challenge.

A review of historical records suggests that although his best engineers failed to solve these problems, Ford failed his engineers as well. As detailed next, Ford did not put aside adequate time to work on the X engine on an extended basis with his engineers. He comes across not only as an interloper but as a confounder by setting up teams of engineers pitted against each other. For a while, the Hungarian-trained engineers competed against the American-trained engineers in an almost social Darwinistic contest of the survival of the fittest. Prototypes from both teams of engineers were built by the same tool shop. When the Hungarians complained that the Americans were receiving an unfair advantage because the American-trained engineers' prototypes were being built with greater alacrity, Ford personally transferred the head of the tool shop. If Ford was attempting to put social Darwinism into practice, the results spoke for themselves. A team effort led by Ford had produced the Model T. With the X engine, Ford's genius was at arm's length, lacked continuity, and too often seemed to hinder rather than synergize the efforts of his engineers.

Many had joined Ford not as much for the opportunity to work with Henry Ford and to change the world (as Ford had already proven he could do), but for the money.

In the 1920s, Ford sought to leave in his wake two failures. His first major public failure was his attempt in January 1916 to stop World War I by chartering the *Oscar*, also dubbed Ford's "Peace Ship." In that effort, Ford spent more than a month aboard the ship, on an unsuccessful odyssey for peace that led him from press conferences to the White House and to Norway. Second, in the 1919 embarrassment of the *Chicago Tribune* trial where Ford sued the newspaper for calling him an "ignorant idealist," the newspaper lost the libel suit and Ford was laughed back to his castle Fair Lane with an award of six cents for damages. The trial also brought about a resolve to show what Ford had meant when he had been quoted in the trial as saying "History is bunk." Ford was distracted—first, by his pursuit of history that helped make his Greenfield Village testament of history come to life, and second, by his "girl Friday," Evangeline Dahlinger. (John Dahlinger was born in 1923. Most people familiar with Henry Ford believe the child was Henry's illegitimate son.) Furthermore, Henry's distaste for financiers led to his festering anti-Semitism that surfaced in his articles in the Ford Motor Company's newspaper, the *Dearborn Independent*. The publication of a series of anti-Semitic articles, including publicizing such pseudo-history as the "Protocols of Zion" by Ford's editor, led to a boycott by Jewish people, resulting in Henry Ford being forced to make a public apology to the Jewish people and to terminate publication of the *Independent*. In light of all these factors, we can envision Ford's impatience with his engineers as they worked to solve the remaining problems with the X engine. The early promise of the engine had faded because of the performance problems of prototypes. By 1925, Model T sales were in a downward slide, if not a precipice. Pressure mounted, and criticism and impatience abounded. Meanwhile, Ford was restoring the Wayside Inn in Massachusetts, beginning in 1923, in practice for his mega-restoration, antique collecting exhibition—the world's largest indoor-outdoor museum and located in Dearborn—that was to open in celebration of the Golden Jubilee of Edison's invention of the light bulb.

Ford was a man on the move. Although he had been a man of great achievement, Ford's many distractions from the core of his business made him at times a hard man for whom to work. That sentiment is well laced through all the engineers who worked at Fair Lane in the Experimental Room or at the old tractor building where the Henry Ford Museum stands today. It is similar to reading a tragic opera to see the drama unfold. The question is: Could Ford have confronted his failures and moved onward, rolling up his sleeves as he did at the eleventh hour with the Model A? If he had done so, could he have solved the problems of the X engine? Or could he have leaped ahead to his triumph of the 1930s, the first V-8 common folks could afford, as he had with the Model T in 1908? The X engine was a bad application for cars. However, many of the V-8 engineers had worked previously on the X engine. The frustrations of the X engine did not top the success of the Model T, but they helped spawn the V-8 a decade later. In a 1956 issue of *Automotive Issues*, author Murray Fahnestock asked, "Isn't the modern V-8 nothing more than the top half of an X?"[2-3]

Another question concerns Ford establishing a competition between the Hungarian- and American-trained engineers. Because one of every two cars was made by Ford and because Ford dominated world markets, external competition was no longer as keen as it had been when Henry Ford had galvanized his team to produce the Model T. The Model T had risen out of raw unbridled competition when literally hundreds of new companies were trying to break into the new auto business after the turn of the century. No doubt Ford felt he could recreate that cauldron of productivity in-house by a "survival of the fittest" approach. When that strategy did not work, trusted engineers such as Allen Horton resigned from Ford and could not be lured back to the company. Once the mechanical tinkerer who worked with others to create miracles, Ford at this point was immersed in dozens of other projects that had caught his eye. He then tinkered with his engineers from a sporadic distance, leaving the fulcrum of his success to fracture and his company's dominance to falter.

One thing that becomes clear in reading these oral histories is that, with all of his triumphs, Ford was quick to put down and challenge anyone having a college degree. Harold Hicks, who had both

bachelor's and master's degrees in engineering from the University of Michigan, took pains to hide his credentials from the elder Ford, including a Tau Beta Pi key (the engineering honorary). When Henry Ford himself received an honorary doctorate degree from the University of Michigan in 1927, his boyhood friend, Dr. Edsel Ruddiman, in a letter needled him that Ruddiman had never pictured Ford as an academic. Perhaps Ford's own feelings of insecurity of not living up to his achievements from 1910 to 1920, which Ruddiman's letter mentions, kept Ford from bringing out the best in his highly talented engineering crews and ultimately cost him the respect of many. Allen Horton was said to have been Henry Ford's right arm and could give form and function to Ford's inspirations of mechanical genius. However, Horton quit and refused the offer of a new car when Ford pleaded with him to remain. Others similar to Harold Hicks eventually were fired and became embittered toward Ford.

When Ford was out of town and not watching his engineers, he was doing creative and fulfilling work. His travels took him to places such as Berry College in Rome, Georgia, his Village Industries program in both the Upper and Lower Peninsulas of Michigan, and his restoration of the Botsford and Wayside Inns of Michigan and Massachusetts, respectively. The frustrations of fouling plugs and burnt out rods were forgotten. Likewise, we could add Henry Ford's initiatives in aviation and overseas expansion, which have made Ford a world-class company to this day. All of these distractions, or perhaps ventures divided, eventually removed the halo from Henry Ford's head and gave him the masque of humanity, with all its glory and bitter disappointments.

Ford's hands-on mechanical genius had caused a revolution in 1908. However, by 1920, his hands were busy with more important things, or he simply was too far ahead of his time. In the 1930s, Ford drove his engineers to do the impossible by designing a way to make a V-8 engine in one cast. Until that time, only the wealthy could afford a V-8. After Ford succeeded, even Clyde Barrow of bank-robbing fame wrote a letter of thanks to him. In 1920, Ford had set out to top his T with the X engine. In 1922, Harold Hicks was transferred, and Eugene Farkas accepted the engineering challenge that was too much for even his genius. In 1927, Ford put aside the X engine development and began work in earnest on an "intermediate" car, the Model A.[2-4] He rolled up his sleeves and spent a lot of time with his son Edsel to bring out the Model A. However, by 1927, people said Henry Ford had waited too long. Ford had fired Edsel's close friend and sister-in-law's husband, Ernest Kanzler, for stating the obvious in a memo: a replacement for the Model T was needed. Ford wanted to improve on the Model T in 1920 when he ordered development of the X engine power plant. He and his engineers worked almost a decade to solve the lubrication and other problems. In the process, Ford acquired a Model T image, which has remained with him to this day. As a result, Ford was forced to scramble to build the Model A, a good car. However, its greatness was in its value, and it never came close to achieving the success of the Ford Model T.

At the dawn of the Roaring Twenties, Ford was a confident man, having wrested full control of his company from his early financial partners. Little did Ford suspect that at the end of the decade, not only would the X engine be termed a failure by almost everyone but himself, but that those who worked with him on the project would have lost much of their respect for him because of his personal failures as well. Allen Horton had been given the assignment of developing the successor to the T when half the auto-driving public drove Fords. In many ways, Horton was similar to another talented Ford engineer— Howard Simpson. Horton left Ford for a successful career with Chrysler, and Simpson went on to invent the Simpson gear set, a key component in modern transmissions. Both were brilliant engineers whose services Ford personally treasured and employed in his Experimental Room work. Both had no problem with Ford being the boss, but they recoiled at how they and their colleagues sometimes were treated and how their leader occasionally acted. Henry Ford had not rested on his laurels. What is worse is that in the 1920s, he had drifted into the perilous waters of anti-Semitism and adultery. Both thwarted Ford's genius and induced those who worked most closely with him during those times to lose respect for the man, if not for his many achievements.

Ford sometimes would have his high-level executives come to the Experimental Room for meetings. After these meetings, he would point out to his engineers what big shots had to come not only at his beck and call, but at the beck and call of an engineer: Henry Ford was one of them. At the same time, Ford occasionally would bring Evangeline Dahlinger to one of the dance practice sessions that he held after 1925 in the south side of the Experimental Room opposite the engineers. Sometimes the workers would be warned to stay away from the old "plumbing shack," with its picture window view of the falls where the boss and his "girl Friday" Evangeline would sometimes meet. In some ways, the top floor of the Experimental Room resembles an eagle's nest astride the thundering falls, and the comings and goings of anyone at the plumbing shack were in full view.

John McIntyre and Floyd Apple, each with twenty-five years of work experience at Fair Lane, shared their observations. I remember John McIntyre, the Scottish immigrant gardener. McIntyre's quiet voice dropped to a whisper of shame for the "old man" that he loved when he responded to a direct question about Ford's relationship to Evangeline. Allen Horton and Howard Simpson are not as direct in their oral histories, but reading between the lines and the testimony of their own actions clearly show that Ford's faithlessness to his calling as an engineer and as a spouse exacted a real price. Historic preservation was the great winner of renown for Ford in the 1920s, outshining in the long run the glitzy and successful launch of the Ford Model A. Ford and his Ford vehicles were famous again, but the Roaring Twenties left Ford's justly deserved fame of the prior decade mixed with the infamy of both personal shortcomings and his almost decade-long quest of the engineering failure, the X engine.

Ford Motor Company had entered the Roaring Twenties by surging to a long head start on worldwide dominance in the auto industry. By the end of the decade, even the popularity and songs of how Henry had made a lady out of Lizzie could not hide the frustrating facts that Ford's engineers saw. The company's early lead and bright future, similar to the founder's personal life, were declining. Ford did surge back with the success of the V-8 in the 1930s, but many felt the early lead had been squandered, and the decline continued until Ford's death. It would be generations until a grandson, Henry Ford II, rescued the corporate side of the company and propelled it back to worldwide profits. However, the company never regained the dominance against General Motors it once had enjoyed. Henry's namesake grandson also worked hard to mend fences with the Jewish people to the extent that some Arabic countries boycotted the purchase of Fords. They did not want to buy cars that may have been built in Israel.

Henry's two great-grandsons—Edsel Ford II and William Clay Ford—inherited the task of restoring respect and admiration per force of their character and moral leadership. It is ironic that their personal leadership of the company came to national attention when the powerhouse their great grandfather had built at the Rouge River blew up with much pain, suffering, and loss of life in February 1999. The behavior of both young Fords helped put a caring, human face on the Ford family leadership again. In the aftermath of this disastrous explosion of Henry Ford I's landmark powerhouse, the renewal of Ford moral and corporate leadership came of age. The powerhouse was a touchstone not only to their great-grandfather but to that decade in which Ford had both the industrial and moral capital to lead a company and the world into a new era. Indeed, Henry Ford took his company and the world into new, uncharted waters. However, the rocks, shoals, and icebergs were and always are waiting to sink or damage the ships of even the greatest of titans.

In the ceiling vents of Henry Ford's beloved powerhouse at Fair Lane, above the state-of-the-art machinery for which Thomas Alva Edison laid the cornerstone, are twin birds or doves of peace. The machinery is massive but clean and simple. There are no Doric columns to symbolize, as had the ornamentation on the ship *Titanic*, that technology was god. John Bowditch, an authority on historic machinery and consultant to the Fair Lane powerhouse restoration, said that after the *Titanic* sunk, powerhouses everywhere were swept clean of technological deification. Howard Simpson and others who knew Henry Ford as a hero of labor with his five-dollar day and the builder of the mighty Rouge with its awesome power plant, as well as the Henry Ford of the Roaring Twenties, felt Ford had perhaps begun to elevate himself to the status of a demigod in which irrational and immoral behavior could not only be rationalized but could be put on exhibition among his closest and most guarded associates. The sinking of the *Titanic* swept Ford's and other contemporary powerhouses clean of Doric columns. The many good things that Ford started in the fields of historic preservation and education, which also began to blossom during this time, served as a wind to sweep in the many positive achievements that were yet to come for the complex and controversial auto king, even at the age of sixty-seven in 1930.

MY NEW MODEL A

Music & Lyrics by Donn Werling

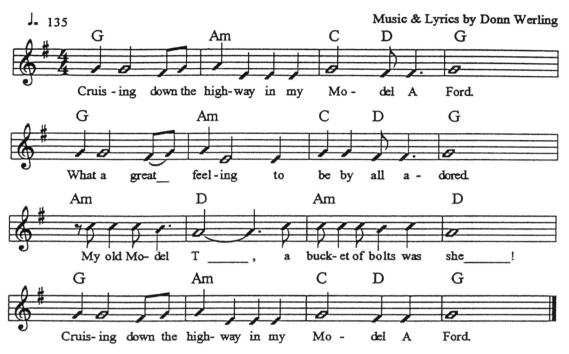

2. Cruising down the highway in my new Model A
What a great feeling to have 4-wheel brakes.
Her curvaceous lines — like Lincoln's, mighty fine;
Cruising down the highway in my new Model A.

3. Cruising down the highway in my Model A Ford,
Wearing my racoon coat and my Wolverine garb.
Down to Notre Dame, Michigan will win this game.
Cruising down the highway in my Model A Ford.

CHAPTER THREE

FAIR LANE: THE RESIDENCE

When Henry Ford moved into Fair Lane in January 1916, he was riding on the first waves of his national and international celebrity status. His fame had not spread because he had become the world's largest builder of automobiles. Rather, he had become a hero of labor and the hope of millions who set sail for America, in part because he paid a wage that not only assured physical survival but through which a laborer could purchase the very things he made, including an automobile.

In January 1916, Ford had just returned from more than a month-long peace odyssey aboard the *Oscar*, which also was dubbed the "Peace Ship" and other less flattering names. His mission had led him from press conferences to the White House and to Norway. The peace trip had been Ford's first major public failure. After making the impossible possible with his Model T, Henry Ford was stunned by the depth of the failure of the trip. Not only had it failed—he had been made a laughingstock of the media. Consumed with matters other than the building of Fair Lane, both at the company and in using his chartered Peace Ship to try to stop a world war, Ford was absent during completion of the residence. During the previous December, Clara and Edsel had moved into what would become Henry and Clara's home for the final thirty-plus years of their lives. Having lost touch with the construction of his family's dream home, Henry Ford was probably was anxious to see it.

1915	Fair Lane completed	1927	Model A introduced; Model T discontinued
	Bought the bungalow in the Upper Peninsula	1929	Greenfield Village/Museum dedicated
1916	Bought home in Ft. Myers	1929–1941	*The Great Depression*
1917	Fordson tractor	1932	Ford V-8
	Birth of Henry Ford II, the first of four grandchildren	1935	Built Richmond Hill
1918	Migratory Bird Treaty with Canada	1937	Battle of the Overpass—U.A.W.
1918–1924	"Four Vagabonds" camping trips	1939–1945	*World War II*
1919	Ford sole owner of Ford Motor Company	1940	Henry Ford II and Anne McDonnell marry
1919–1927	X engine (The engine/car that never was)	1941	First plastic car (soybeans)
1921	First met Martha Berry		Ford signs with the U.A.W.
1922	Lincoln Motor Company purchased		Birth of Charlotte Ford, first great-grandchild
1924	Built first diesel freighters on the Great Lakes	1943	Death of Edsel Ford
1925	Admitted to Huron Mt. Club	1947	Death of Henry Ford
	Began acquiring Georgia land	1948	Edsel Ford II born to Mr. and Mrs. Henry Ford II
1926	Ford Tri-motor	1950	Death of Clara Ford

Named after the road to the fairgrounds in County Cork, Ireland, from where his ancestors emigrated, Ford's Irish-American castle known as Fair Lane was located in County Wayne, Michigan. The huge structure cost ten times more than Henry had budgeted. The castle was largely Clara's, whose ancestors were from Warwick, where they lived in the shadow of the large and famous castle of the same name in England. When Henry Ford walked into Fair Lane for the first time, having been gone for months trying to stop World War I, his first remark to the architect was, "...and you call this a home?" (Photograph from the Archives of the Henry Ford Estate. Balthazar Korab, photographer.)

Original plans for the home called for the expenditure of slightly less than a quarter-million dollars in 1915. Actual expenses eventually totaled much more than two million dollars. Ford had fired the first architect, after having to put the kibosh on a *Detroit News* story that told of the marble palace Ford was building in Dearborn. Ford then turned to William Van Tine, a Pittsburgh architect noted primarily as an interior designer. Van Tine seized the opportunity and drove himself mercilessly to achieve the state of perfection he had designed for his client. Ed Lusk, now deceased university colleague of mine and a former employee at the Henry Ford Museum, recalls Henry Ford's first reaction to his new home, as told to him by Van Tine.

"And you call this a home?" said Ford, standing in the main entrance hall and leaning backward to take in the 25-foot-tall, 30-foot by 20-foot hall and stairway. Ford must have wondered how many architects he had to fire to get his message across.

To find one another in the enormous structure, Henry and Clara used to sing out bird whistles to each other. Perhaps only the log cabin room of the house met with Henry's favor. He had seen enough of reception rooms and the size of the first floor. Henry even kept a bike at the front entrance of the residence and once used it to get from one side of the residence to the other.

Walking down the marble stairs into the marble hallway, electric lights cast a glow resembling the light in a castle or a dungeon. The *Detroit News* had called the place a marble castle. Ford would not permit Clara to have a lot of servants, though. He did not want servants hovering over him to see whether or not he ate the potato skins.

Walking into the warmth of the log-lined Field Room, with its field-stone fireplace that holds a blazing fire, is a dramatic transition from princely elegance to peasant style. Ford needed the room here for the fiddler and for dancing. It is one of the largest rooms in the house, but here the log walls and the fireplace give out warmth. Off the back of the Field Room, Henry had a secret closet built in which to do his watchmaking. The Field Room's secret closet also was a handy place in which to escape when he needed the privacy that the large rooms on the first floor ill afforded.

The Library: You Are What You Read

It has been widely written and reported that Henry Ford, with only an eighth-grade education, was not much of a reader. However, others who reported seeing their uncle and great-uncle almost a fixture of reading on the Estate's sunporch give a different and firsthand set of observations on how Henry Ford explored the world around him. Certainly Ford was a kinesthetic learner, but he also loved to read or being read to by Clara.

Richly carved hazel oak surrounds three sides of the library, framing a view of the entrance to Fair Lane. One-thousand leatherbound volumes line the walls—the history of mankind as selected by Henry and Clara Ford. The library of the Estate primarily held "show" books, which were selected by Clara more for the appearance of their bindings than for their reading. Many of the books described in the next several paragraphs came from Ford's personal library and were scattered throughout Fair Lane and his office, rather than on the shelves of the Estate library.

Ford's library books are filled with his markings, and the notations on the books suggest he was as wide ranging in thought as he was in action. Some books seem almost current by their titles: *God in the Public Schools* and *America and a New World Order*. Others have a classic flavor to them, reflecting Ford's love of northern Michigan and his interest in Henry Wadsworth Longfellow. The latter celebrated in poetry two of Ford's prized possessions: a quarter-million acres of the land of Hiawatha in Michigan's Upper Peninsula, and the Wayside Inn in South Sudbury, Massachusetts.

Of course, there were obvious biases. Mechanical and engineering texts are well represented, but the biggest single consumer of shelf space is Ford's twenty-three-volume collection of the complete works of the naturalist, John Burroughs. Furthermore, Ford had two com-

The library at Fair Lane was more for show than for reading. Newspapers and comics were more likely to be read here in the library. The Fords had hundreds of other books—many the gifts of authors—tucked away in various bookcases and offices where their real reading occurred. The books include personal notes from the authors, some begging for financial support from the Fords. One note in Ford's handwriting said that "three things, my friend, are needed for success: patience, persistence, and integrity." (Photograph from the Collections of Henry Ford Estate. Manning Bros. Collection)

plete sets of these volumes. One set was autographed by Burroughs, with the words: "To Henry Ford, who has given a new breath of life to so many of his fellow beings." The date of the autograph is 1915—two years after Ford had succeeded, with the help of Thomas Edison, his Ford dealers, and school children, in passing the Weeks-McLean Migratory Bird Act, which laid the groundwork for the Migratory Bird Treaty of 1918 between the United States and Canada. For the first time in world history, as far as I can determine, laws and treaties between two countries stopped the slaughter of "...other fellow beings."

John Burroughs sometimes has been called the "backyard naturalist" or "John of birds." His writings helped the cause of conservation as much or perhaps even more than the actions of John Muir, founder of the Sierra Club. Henry Ford was but one of millions whose love of nature was enflamed with Burroughs' writings because Burroughs wrote about what the common man could see and enjoy, which was as much endangered as the mountains of John Muir.

Not all of the books have as direct a connection to a Ford hero or a Ford cause, but many do. One of the thickest books is a copy of the *Congressional Record*. In its voluminous pages, one paragraph on one page is highlighted. The paragraph states that someday the strong arm of the government will throw its arms around the financial interests that have been exploiting the farmer. Henry Ford was not only born and raised on a farm; he was one of the world's biggest farmers with more than 12,000 acres in production. More importantly, this highlighted paragraph is a touchstone to both Ford's and Michigan's greenback dollar history. Farmers never had much respect for financiers or railroad interests because together these two groups often worked to exploit agriculture as much as to serve it.

The roots of this antipathy can be traced to Ireland, particularly to the great potato famine and the loss of ancient farm holdings to the wealthy. At that time, the reserves of the wealthy enabled them to not only ride out the tragedy, but to expand their holdings when Ford's ancestors had little choice but to emigrate or starve. Thus, the seeds of the Michigan greenback dollar revolution were born in Europe, and experience with the banks and railroad interests provided the seed bed for the anti-Semitism that flowered in rural Michigan areas and in Henry Ford. The tragedy was that in Henry Ford's mind, any Jewish person and a financier were one and the same, and the highlighted paragraph in the *Congressional Record* speaks volumes about his attitude. Ford was a grade-school-educated farmer who changed the world, but he never outgrew the provincialism and biases of his region or his century. He lived more than half his life in the twentieth century; however, in many respects, Ford had a nineteenth-century *Weltanschauung*, or "world view."

The Man Who Talks with the Flowers[3-1] is a slender volume in Ford's collection. It is the story of the man who in many ways took the place of Thomas Edison after the inventor's death in 1931. George Washington Carver was a *bona fide* Ph.D. of national and international acclaim. Ford never felt uncomfortable with the professor from Tuskegee Institute as he did with other academics, and perhaps the title of the slender volume implies why. If Ford was once and always a farmer, then to walk through a field with Carver by his side, sampling the weeds, was the most natural thing to do. Furthermore, similar to Ford, Carver focused his concerns on the plight of the common farmer. Austin Curtis, Dr. Carver's assistant, said that he never heard a cross word between the two men, but that an intensity of conversation grew naturally from shared convictions and hands-on commitment to helping the plight of the rural poor.

If Carver took Edison's spot in Henry Ford's life as the years passed, then Jack Miner, the Canadian naturalist, took the place of John Burroughs. Because Ford became friends with Burroughs and Miner about the same time, it might be better to suggest that when Burroughs died, Jack Miner and his family helped fill the void. Miner's autobiography is one of the first wildlife photo-essay books. It uses many photographs that came originally from Henry Ford's photographic crews, whose documentary film footage provided the core attraction for Jack Miner becoming the first international interpreter of our wildlife heritage.

Two four-foot-long shelves of the library at Fair Lane are devoted entirely to God. Most are traditional titles on how to use the Bible. Ford, who took a pledge with President Woodrow Wilson to read the Bible every day, no doubt found the guides helpful. A half-dozen titles remain which reflect Ford's interest in reincarnation, an interest that perhaps stemmed from his dedication to humility. Ford could not explain how, in his own lifetime, he had done so much; thus, he desired to pass the credit to those who came before him. Whether this view of Ford is true or not depends largely on how you read his comments on the matter. Certainly the books in his library suggest that at least for a time during his life, like the titles of the books in his library, Ford was an ardent explorer of *The Mansions of the Soul*. Missing from the collection now housed at Fair Lane are the many antique Bibles that the Fords collected during their lifetimes. The Bibles either were sold at auction or remain with the family in spiritual lineage with their famous forebear who took the time to seek God.

Behind books on nature, books on God, self-help books on health, and books on mechanical engineering, the titles on war and money are most prolific. Some of the titles seem contemporaneous, with libertarian concerns about big government. *The Cost of Government in the US 1928–29* would need only to have its title updated by seven decades. The titles suggest both a right- and left-wing mentality.

Perhaps in Ford's mind, both perspectives wrapped around and touched in the back of anyone's thinking where the basic survival functions and the creative problem-solving components of the mind meet. I am reminded of the incongruity of Henry Ford listening to Kay Cushman, the valedictorian, speak at a Fordson high-school graduation. After the speech, Ford congratulated the young woman who had berated the evils of capitalism, with the words that she had many good points in her Depression-era valedictory. Ever the complex personality, Ford's books reflect a diversity of views, ranging from mainstream to a stream running uphill. Ford has *How to Win Friends and Influence People* by Dale Carnegie; *The Prophet*, by Kahlil Gibran; and Rudolph Steiner's *The Philosophy of Spiritual Activity*. All these books sit side by side on Ford's shelf.

Ford was born during the battle of Gettysburg. He has been quoted as saying that, at least for a time, he thought perhaps he was a reincarnated soldier. Although the number of books on the Civil War in Ford's personal library do fill a shelf, most are about the life of Abraham Lincoln, and one is about Lincoln's mother, Nancy Hanks. Perhaps Ford identified more with Lincoln the Great Emancipator and less with the fallen soldier. Similar to Lincoln, Ford had lost his mother in an untimely fashion. (She died in childbirth.) Both Lincoln and Ford were products of the Midwest and its rustic schools of the period. However, each had a dedicated sense of purpose and conviction. This is not to disclaim the historical footnote that Ford at one time perhaps thought he was a reincarnated Civil War soldier from the battle of Gettysburg. Rather, it shows what solace and inspiration the life of Lincoln was for Ford, as it has been to so many others. Lincoln was labeled a loser but achieved success late in life. When getting started, Ford was called "crazy Henry" and worse. Similar to Lincoln, Ford achieved his pinnacle of success late in life. In 1923, Ford bought the Lincoln Motor Company. Most reports say the purchase was made at Edsel's behest because of Edsel's interest in the Lincoln Motor Company reputation for fine styling. Perhaps there also was a tinge of covetousness in Ford—not so much for the reputation for styling, but for the Lincoln name. In many ways, Ford viewed himself as the great emancipator of the masses and, in particular, the farmer. Thus, it was easy for Ford to agree to Edsel's wish of having a Lincoln being the marquee vehicle over a Ford.

The Ford Motor Company publication, the *Dearborn Independent*, was famous for the folk wisdom of *Mr. Ford's Page*. However, it also was infamous for the anti-Semitic republication of some of the worst pseudo-history in the annals of humankind. The *Dearborn Independent*, "the chronicler of the neglected truth," had sprinkled through the pages of its issues during the early 1920s a venom that should have led to the questioning of its source. From these issues, many biographers generally have concluded that Ford was a virulent anti-Semite, at least during the period of his greatest fame and power in the early 1920s. Few have explored or probed the underlying causes for this tincture that spoiled this otherwise folksy publication, ultimately leading to the demise of the newspaper and a formal apology from Henry Ford to the Jewish community.

The actions deemed anti-Semitic were those not only of Henry Ford but of his assistants as well. Recent oral history from Wilbur Donaldson, one of Ford's personal drivers whose father was an associate editor at the newspaper, substantiates this view. Donaldson stated that his father blamed much of the anti-Semitism on W.J. Cameron, the editor of the *Dearborn Independent*, and on Liebold, the pro-German personal secretary of Mr. Ford. Donaldson's father felt that they took Ford's ignorance and bias against Jewish financiers and used it to push the sometimes anti-Semitic lines of the newspaper to the breaking point. Ultimately, neither Ford nor his neighbor and friend, the Rabbi Leo Franklin, would tolerate publication of the *Dearborn Independent* any longer. At a national news conference, with the Rabbi at his side, Ford issued an apology to the Jewish people and directed the publication to make a quiet exit.

Text of Henry Ford's Apology to the Jewish People

For some time I have given consideration to the series of articles concerning Jews which since 1920 have appeared in the Dearborn Independent. *Some of them have been reprinted in pamphlet form under the title "The International Jew." Although public publications are my property, it goes without saying that in the multitude of my activities, it has been impossible for me to devote personal attention to their management or to keep informed as to their contents. It has therefore inevitably followed that the conduct and policies of [my] publications had to be delegated to men whom I placed in charge of them and upon whom I relied implicitly.*

To my great regret, I have learned that Jews generally, and particularly those of this country, not only resent these publications as promoting anti-Semitism, but regard me as their enemy. Trusted friends with whom I have conferred recently have assured me in all sincerity that in their opinion the character of the charges and insinuations made against the

Jews, both individually and collectively, contained in many of the articles that have been circulated periodically in the Dearborn Independent *and have been reprinted in the pamphlets mentioned, justifies the righteous indignation entertained by Jews everywhere toward me because of the mental anguish occasioned by the unprovoked reflections made upon them.*

This has led me to direct my personal attention to the subject, in order to ascertain the exact nature of these articles. As a result of this survey, I confess I am deeply mortified that this journal, which is intended to be constructive and not destructive, has been made the medium for resurrecting exploded fictions, for giving currency to the so-called Protocols of the Wise Men of Zion, which have been demonstrated, as I learn, to be gross forgeries, and for contending that the Jews have been engaged in a conspiracy to control the capital and the industries of the world, besides laying at their door many offenses against decency, public order, and good morals.

Had I appreciated even the general nature, to say nothing of the details, of these utterances, I would have forbidden their circulation without a moment's hesitation. I deem it my duty as an honorable man to make amends for the wrong done to the Jews as fellow-men and brothers, by asking their forgiveness for the harm that I have unintentionally committed, by retracting so far as lies within my power the offensive charges laid at their door by these publications, and by giving them the unqualified assurance that henceforth they may look to me for friendship and good will. [3-2]

Henry Ford

Despite Ford's efforts to make amends, this remains as perhaps the greatest blot on a lifetime of achievement, which for the most part practiced equal opportunity. Ford had helped lead the way in hiring minorites at equal wages, and he demonstrated that people with handicaps and people of all ethnic groups and creeds—including thousands of Jewish, Arabic, and African Americans—could work together to create one of the richest and most successful premier corporations of all time.[3-3]

Perhaps one of the most dramatic days at Fair Lane was when Henry Ford returned from his news conference in which he apologized to the Jewish people. By his side had been his old neighbor from the Boston-Edison[3-4] days, the esteemed Rabbi Leo Franklin, who was a prominent leader in the reformed Jewish movement for many years.

Ford probably reflected to himself as he sank into the chair opposite the blue couch on which a copy of the *Dearborn Independent* lay. What a grilling Ford must have endured! It had been like the Peace Ship debacle—a personally humiliating experience—and all because of a few articles in a newspaper. Ford probably wondered where his First Amendment rights were then? The *Chicago Tribune* got off the hook of Ford's defamation lawsuit with a six-cent fine in 1919, after using outright lies to blaspheme Ford's reputation. Now, eight years later, Ford had become subject to a personal and national boycott simply because, or at least most likely in Ford's view, his editor became carried away with Ford's campaign to educate the public on the origins and current evils of finance and the financiers. Even the March 3 *Congressional Record*, a copy of which is in Ford's library and contains Ford's notations, cited how financial interests were exploiting the farmer. Ford must have felt he was the farmer's spokesman. When he as a farmer spoke up, he was called a bigot, even by old friends. Ford blamed this on the power of Jewish (financial) interests, which he viewed as Communists working to control and enslave his company and his country. If Ford had run for and obtained the presidency of the United States, then as the *Congressional Record* states, the great ring of restraint of the government would have at last been thrown around the financiers.

The editor of the *Dearborn Independent* was a hard-working and efficient German-American with Fascist tendencies. Ford admired the German people, and the facist movement could have been rationalized as a response to the financial manipulations that their economy was forced to endure, both during and after the war. Even the Jewish organizers of the Ford's Peace Ship had indicted their own people, according to Harry Bennett's *We Never Called Him Henry* biography of Henry Ford. Financiers of any stripe were Jewish in Henry Ford's book, although Ford's naturalist friend, John Burroughs, once corrected him. On one of their camping trips, Edison and Ford were railing on about Jay Gould and the shylocks who "stole" most of the money made on Edison's light bulb, then added insult to injury by dropping Edison's name from the General Electric Company, the same as J.P. Morgan likely wanted to do to Ford when Henry Ford was financing the multimillion-dollar buyout of non-Ford stockholders. Ford had kicked J.P. Morgan out of his house, and Clara Ford reportedly was upset with her husband's rudeness! Ford could easily identify with Edison's anger at Jay Gould and company—who Edison and Ford perceived as being a Jewish robber baron. Then, the normally soft-spoken Burroughs could not take any more and said, "Jay Gould and his friends are all Presbyterians!"[3-5]

Ford must have regretted that his old neighbor and friend, Dr. Franklin, had to become embroiled in this. To lose his friendship and respect after all these years was troubling to Henry. Perhaps Dr. Franklin was a wise and true friend by bringing this to a head before things became inflammatory. Who knows where Liebold and his pro-German sympathizers would have led Ford? Perhaps the company and all Ford's far-flung endeavors had grown out of control. On one hand, Ford never regretted having raised the issue because in Henry Ford's mind, finance and who controls it were the biggest stumbling blocks to progress and production. However, Henry Ford stood by the apology Dr. Franklin and his aides prepared. In Ford's parlance, financiers and Jews were always one one and the same: J.P. Morgan, Jay Gould, the DuPonts, or the Rothchilds—Christian or Jew—Ford never cared if a person's race or religion was different than his own.[3-6] Ford always appreciated the man himself. "As for money, it should be the servant, not the master."[3-7]

The following two historic ballads illustrate the degree of variance in public sentiment regarding Henry Ford. In one song, Ford is the hero; in the other, he is the apologist. Biographers and balladeers are still sorting out the many virtues and contradictions of the often controversial Henry Ford.

"Help the Other Fellow" Henry Ford

(Can be sung to the tune of "Marching Through Georgia")

Words by Edward Marshall (1915)
Music by Louis Iungerich Matthews

Verse 1

There's a cer-tain rule to go by, and it's gold-en in its hue,

It's that help-ing oth-er fel-lows is the wis-est thing to do;

Hate your neigh-bor and your la-bor will be mul-ti-plied by two,

But just help the oth-er fel-low, and it will come right back to you.

Verse 2

As you jour-ney on life's high-way, now and then you will get stuck,

For no per-son ev-er trod it who com-plete-ly dodged hard luck;

And your neigh-bor's help-ful la-bor will come han-dy when you're blue,

If you've helped the oth-er fel-low, it will come right back to you.

Verse from "Since Henry Ford Apologized to Me"

Written by Billy Rose (1927)

I was sad and I was blue,

But now I'm just as good as you

Since Hen-ry Ford a-pol-o-gized to me.

I've thrown a-way my lit-tle Chev-ro-let

And bought my-self a Ford Cou-pe.

I told the Sup-'rin-ten-dant that

the Dearborn In-de-pen-dent

Does-n't have to hang up where it used to be.

I'm glad he changed his point of view

And I even like Edsel, too,

The Formal Dining Room at Fair Lane

The dining room at Fair Lane is perhaps the greatest achievement of the architect William Van Tine. It is Palladian balance achieved to perfection, using the finest materials and craftsmanship available. The large room also contains a less formal alcove that overlooks the blue garden, where the Fords frequently dined with each other, with grandchildren, or with guests. The blue garden was Mrs. Ford's favorite, with numerous shades of blue flowers with white and yellow accents. The table of state in the main portion of the room spreads beneath a large silver chandelier, and the colonial symbol of welcome—a pineapple—is its bottom-most pendant. The walls and furniture are done in one of the rarest of woods—rose leaf mahogany. Its rich brown tones set a standard of elegance unmatched in the remainder of the fifty-six-room residence. The woodcarving and plasterwork make the room one of the most elegant dining rooms in the world. The woodcarvers were from Germany, and many were recent immigrants. They had come to America in part because they could make five dollars a day building cars for Henry Ford, which was two to three times the wage they made at home practicing their ancient craft. Quite simply, Ford had some of the best craftsmen in the world come to work at Ford Motor Company. Thus, it was a simple task for his people to assemble the more than six-hundred workmen who succeeded in building Fair Lane in less than two years.

It is hard to imagine anyone, much less Henry Ford, riding his bicycle into this formal setting. However, Henry did just that, with a bottle of wine tucked under each arm. (Photograph from the Archives of the Henry Ford Estate. Manning Brothers, photographers)

We can only imagine the thoughts of Henry Ford, his guests, and his family relations as they dined, while taking in the egg and dart symbols of ancient Greece which represented life and death. These symbols are carved more than nine hundred times into a frieze that circles the entire room. Wooden garlands of flowers drape each doorway, carved relief-style into the wood of the door, window posts, and lintels, swirling so delicately that it seems as if the rush of wind from an open window could send them swinging in celebration.

One day, in the dining room at Fair Lane, Clara and Henry Ford were having dinner with members of the Bryant family, including one of Clara's favorite nieces, Grace Prunk, upon whose oral history this account is based. Ford would have been seated at one end of the large mahogany table, taking in the scene of Clara and her favorite Bryant family members, and perhaps thinking to himself that the room was truly Clara's. Her portrait hung above the elegantly carved sideboard. Her family, the Bryants, were regulars here at the Ford table. Clara enjoyed her family more than Henry enjoyed his own, which in one sense is to be expected. Ford always felt that it was important to keep a distance from relations for business reasons—the thought that Clara avoided Henry's family simply because they were Irish certainly rubbed Henry's brothers and cousins the wrong way. In Henry's book, it should not matter if you came from the most bedeviled country in the world; had two eyes or one; had one foot or none; or were black, white, or red. One man's sweat was as good as another's, according to Henry. Ford even invited his tractor mechanic to lunch to obtain his perspective on how the Fordson tractor held up under use.

Clara's family had been with Clara and Henry when they struggled in Detroit through two failed Ford car ventures. They certainly grew closer because of their struggles together. Her family also had been more inclined to "take a bone and run with it," as had been done by Clara's brother, H.H., in Idaho. Ford sent him a Fordson tractor and a few dollars to help him establish his Ford dealership, but it was an investment that was returned many times. H.H. sold Fords, not Bryants, after all.

At this dinner, Clara probably suggested to Henry from across the table, "Wouldn't a nice glass of sherry go well with this meal?"

At Clara's cue, Henry left the table and exited the room, closing the large, smoothly sliding doors behind him. He was gone quite a long time and then suddenly reappeared at the elegant sliding door entrance, astride a bicycle with two bottles of wine underneath his arms. Keeping his bicycle on the front porch made it handy for Henry to do errands such as this.

Henry Ford sometimes is portrayed to be a male Carrie Nation with his anti-alcoholic prejudices. However, with Clara, who liked an occasional glass of wine and Rolling Rock beer, Ford either made an exception or was much less of an extremist than some have suggested.[3-8]

The Living Room

Almost one thousand square feet of space appears enormous when walking into it from the main entrance hall, as the eye flows into the sunporch and through two walls of windows to the riverscape beyond. It is a room in which many historic introductions and conversations took place. Once in the room, the centerpiece becomes the beautiful gray sienna marble fireplace. On an embossed brass plate, installed by Ford to stop smoke from peeling back into the room, the words of Ralph Waldo Emerson are inscribed from his essay on friendship:

> If I were sure of thee, sure of thy capacity, true to match my words with thine, I would never again think of trifles.

Clara Ford once said that she never objected when her husband put his feet on a fine chair or table and left a scratch in it. Nothing in the house was too good to use. Home was not a showplace; rather, it was a place in which to live and a place to enjoy.

Although their son Edsel lived less than a year at Fair Lane, he was always in the hearts of Clara and Henry Ford. Over the years, Henry's love for his son never faltered. However, the twists and turns of life and differing personalities and preferences led not only to conflict, but to the unresolved conflict that comes from intransigent beliefs and norms, as well as generational shifts. The Emerson quote on the fireplace is particularly insightful. It is flanked and lifted heavenward by two of the most beautiful angels human hands could divine. These angels bespeak Henry Ford's high esteem for Emerson, whose depths Henry plumbed with his naturalist friend, John Burroughs. Burroughs had given Ford a personal tour of Emerson sites on a New England visit. Henry revered Emerson almost as he revered God. Many have said that Emerson's essay, "On Compensation," had the greatest effect on Henry Ford. Excerpts from it resemble the philosophical underpinnings of social Darwinism more than the transcendental movement of which Emerson was at the center.

Most people could identify with many things in that essay, such as the phrase, "Great men are always willing to be little." However, the applications of other passages are not so easily discerned, as in the following:

Not until we are pricked and stung and sorely shot at, awakens the indignation which arms itself with the secret forces…Whilst he sits on the cushion of advantages, he goes to sleep. When he is pushed, tormented, defeated, he has a chance to learn something.

One of the most frequently asked questions by senior visitors to Fair Lane is how Henry could have been so hard on his son. The main freeway in Detroit, I-94, is named the Edsel Ford Freeway in testimony of Edsel's almost universal affection among those who knew him. The concern of most self-made people is that their children will sit on the cushion of their parents' success. Many of the acts of Henry Ford cannot be attributed solely to the philosophy of the great American thinker Ralph Waldo Emerson. Some might be attributed to the literary naturalist from New England, John Burroughs. A little bit of knowledge can be dangerous, and Ford's interpretations of the above-mentioned words from "On Compensation" can perhaps partially explain how Henry Ford chose to *prick* and *prod* and *defeat* his son on so many occasions.

Henry Ford loved to sit in front of a roaring fire in the living room at Fair Lane. Multimillionaire Clara Ford would sit next to him, probably darning socks. Clara, like Henry, was a hands-on personality type who never wanted to let go of gardening or darning. Perhaps Henry asked Callie (Ford's nickname for Clara) to listen to these words from Emerson's essay, "On Compensation":

This is the living room of the house at Fair Lane. A George Inness painting, "The Meadow with Figures," once hung above the main fireplace in perfect consonance with the great meadow Jens Jensen designed to greet the Fords and their guests at the main entrance. Both were masterpieces of the dance of light and shadow. (Photograph from the Archives of the Henry Ford Estate. Edward L. Bryant Collection)

Our strength grows out of our weakness. Not until we are pricked and stung and sorely shot at, awakens the indignation which arms itself with secret forces. A great man is always willing to be little. Whilst he sits on the cushion of advantages, he goes to sleep. When he is pushed, tormented, defeated, he has a chance to learn something; he has been put on his wits, on his manhood; he has gained facts; learns his ignorance; is cured of the insanity of conceit; has got moderation and real skill.

These are words that expressed Henry's feelings toward his son Edsel and the influence of the Kanzlers (Edsel's in-laws) and the society set. Henry knew Edsel was never conceited, but he sought to awaken the indignation of Edsel's soul. Ford did not want Edsel to sink into repose on the cushions of advantages that could prove fleeting. Too much too soon can lead to too little will being mustered. Did Ford know some people thought he was cruel when it came to the way he treated Edsel? Whether he knew this or not, Ford did not shrink from his perceived role or duty. He believed Edsel must learn how tough the world is and must be prepared and fully "armed" to carry the family enterprise forward.

Edsel Ford did not thrive under his father's treatment of him. Many even say it was Edsel's death knell. Whether it was the X engine (whose attributes Henry pursued for almost a decade before abandoning the task and producing the Model A with Edsel) or the preparation of Edsel to meet the challenge of leadership, Ford was persistent to a fault. Edsel—the designer whose grace and artistic abilities are memorialized in the Lincoln and the Model A—was not responsive to being "pricked and stung and sorely shot at." His life and the lives of those who loved him were affected in more traditional ways. His friends and supporters, such as his brother-in-law Ernest Kanzler, were fired. Many felt that Edsel's health and outlook suffered the greatest toll. It was a tragedy that, in the end, fell upon "the old man" himself, and perhaps lost in it all was Ford's zest to live to the age of one hundred.

In Harry Bennett's biography, Ford's service department manager related that he was asked what he would have done if Henry Ford had ever given him the "Emerson" treatment. Bennett quickly replied that he would have fought back. Ford pronounced that is what he wanted Edsel to do—perhaps to arm Edsel with "secret forces" and to give him "real skill" in steering the corporate ship of state as Emerson promised would result. In the end, it was a real-life Shakespearean tragedy, which ennobled Edsel to many as the dutiful son and made Henry appear as a father who dealt with the devil. Ford had taken the wisdom of Emerson too literally. It is possible the convolutions of Emerson were more than an eighth-grade education could wisely interpret.

What could be considered a counterpointed footnote to all this is one that Grace Prunk told about how Clara Ford came to paint the exquisite wood and carvings of the living room. Much to Henry Ford's chagrin, this occurred when Ford was away on one of his field trips. Grace recalled that in a conversation with Clara, she overheard Edsel's wife Eleanor Clay suggest to Clara that the living room appeared outdated and dark and would benefit by being painted a light color. "Everyone is painting their old woodwork these days," and that is what Clara did. In many ways, the relationship between Eleanor and her mother-in-law was the antithesis of the relationship between Edsel and his father. Eleanor, a recognized leader of Detroit fashion and society, had no reservations about sharing and asserting her tastes and opinions. Eleanor did this to an even greater degree after Edsel died and the struggle for the company ensued. Clara became an ally in change where Henry Ford resisted many of Edsel's suggestions in fashion and style.

Most visitors smile when hearing the painted woodwork story. At that time, Henry Ford had walked away from Clara, muttering the words, "Peace at any price." It was a double *entendre* in more ways than one. Someday, if current restoration plans are followed, the living room will be returned to its early 1920s French-grained walnut appearance, the restoration reference period of the site. Historic homes are becoming less rigid about restoration reference periods, and the case could certainly be made that the painted woodwork paints an even more valued historic picture of the two generations of Fords that founded the company and made it a family affair for decades.

The Main Entrance Hall Landing

If the size and ostentatiousness of the main entrance hall were not of Henry's liking, the sayings engraved on his favorite clock and windows certainly must have been. Both reflect the pressure that each minute presents to high-performance people—a symphony lost, an invention not invented, a service not rendered. The grandfather clock, sitting on the landing, perched atop a mountain of stairs, bespeaks the importance of time from a distance. Father Time presides on the peak of the clock, watching the sun's rays of another day slant into the window. The phases of the moon are displayed graphically on the clock, with the time, month, and day of the week. Inscribed are the words:

Slowly, surely, always on, regrets are vain when time is gone.

The 15-foot by 18-foot sunrise-facing window wall has a sundial theme of peasants planting, harvesting, and plowing through the seasons of the year. The words that were chosen also are from a saying commonly used for sundials in England:

To no one is given
Right of delay
Noted in heaven
Passeth each day
Be not thou fruitless
Work while you may
Trifling were bootless[3-9]
Watch thou and pray.

To visitors, these blend with the hallmarks each craftsman carved at the top of the oak wainscoating that rises to the top of the second-story level. Although in the tradition of Europe, they resemble neon signs to the students of Ford. No one except God had the right to stop the sun. Work must continue in its ancient daily tradition. No one had the "right to delay," including the right to strike. Thus, envision the scene of Henry Ford returning to work on a spring day in 1941.

On that day, Henry Ford entered the main entrance hall at Fair Lane and let out his usual bird whistle for Clara Ford. Clara whistled in reply from the upstairs bedroom, and both walked toward each other, meeting at the landing by the clock and window.

In his book, *My Forty Years with Ford*,[3-10] Charles Sorenson recalled the result of that meeting. Clara Ford told Henry she made up her mind. She wanted Ford to sign a contract with the unions and give them the best contract they ever had. Henry was (and Clara wanted him to remain) a hero of the men who worked for him, rather than the villain that the press made him and Harry Bennett out to be.

Henry was concerned about Clara's decision because more than a contract with labor was at stake. He felt that the Communists and social democrats were intent on taking control of Ford. What convinced Henry was the ultimatum that Clara gave to him. If Henry did not do as Edsel and the Michigan governor were saying, then she—Henry's wife of fifty-three years—would publicly leave him.

According to "Cast-Iron" Charlie Sorenson, Henry Ford came into the office the next day and directed Sorenson to settle with the unions and to

In the main entrance hall, Fair Lane's primary billboard proclaims the value of work and the relentless march of time, declaring that only God has the right to stop to the sun. It is perhaps the most insightful space that relates Henry Ford's Weltanschauung, or "world view." Not only is it what is said, but it is how it is said. A nineteenth-century hall with Ford's prized clock surmounted by Father Time echoes the refrains of the stained-glass window: "Slowly, surely, always on, regrets are vain when time is gone" (on the clock). "To no one is given the right of delay" (on the window). (Photograph from the Collections of the Henry Ford Estate)

give them the best contract they ever had. When Sorenson asked Henry what had changed his mind, Henry repeated Clara's threat and ended the conversation with, "What (else) could I do?" It was not a question.

Another story surrounding the clock is much more humorous and gives insight into the value Ford placed upon his watch and clock collection and wildlife. Clem Davis, Henry Ford's watchmaker and tool shop curator in the powerhouse, told the story to Tom Eurich, who for a time owned the clock from the main entrance hall. Clem had Henry Ford's complete confidence. For the Experimental Room, Clem could buy tools that would cost more than $30,000 in 1999 dollars. However, the head gardener, Alphonse De Caluwe, struggled to obtain materials on time for the gardens for Mrs. Ford, who was very tight with money. In addition to his work in the top floor as a toolmaker and watchmaker, Clem had the duty of winding and caring for the clocks in the residence.

In this situation, Henry Ford was reading in his favorite wicker chair on the sunporch. Clem Davis was servicing the grandfather clock on the landing, when he accidentally dropped one of the weights. The weight resounded with a "Clap!" through the bottom of the ornate, eight-foot-tall clock, as if a gun had been fired. Henry Ford rushed from the sunporch toward Clem, who was standing on the landing beside the clock, and yelled, "Clem! Someone is outside shooting my deer!" Clem replied, "Right, Mr. Ford. You go around the meadow way, and I'll go the other way."

The following historical occurrence was relayed by Genevieve Gillette, who was Jens Jensen's landscape assistant, portraying an argument over an ancient oak that was in the direct path of the construction of Fair Lane Drive, circa the summer of 1915. Jensen had given strict orders to his foreman that if Henry Ford had any problem with his design of jogging the drive around an old bur oak, Jensen was to be summoned from Chicago.

Fair Lane Drive. Here was the site of Ford's daily bicycle ride from the north gate on Ford Road to Michigan Avenue. Birds, children, and deer were his favorite sights. (Photograph from the Collections of Henry Ford Museum & Greenfield Village)

Jensen had arrived via train from Chicago to meet with Henry Ford, and the two men stood together on Fair Lane Drive before the ancient oak. Jensen, who had a charismatic way of dealing with scions of industry, spoke on behalf of the ancient oak. Jensen said that this oak was of the bur or prairie variety that had first greeted the French explorer, Cadillac, when he became the first white person to paddle up the Rouge River.

Ford agreed that it was an old tree, but his practical side suggested that in a few years, the tree would be dead and the crook in the road would have to be straightened. That would mean Ford would pay extra to go around tree at this time, and then extra later to straighten the road when the tree died.

Jensen had not come all the way from Chicago to give up so easily, and perhaps he used his experience with a Chicago meat packer to good effect. When Jensen had designed the entrance road to the home for the Armours of meat-packing fame, he included as many gentle curves as possible. He felt that the owner's return home should be in preparation for domestic life, leaving business life behind him. Therefore, Ford should not view this as a crook in the road that would delay his return; rather, Ford should see it as a vista of an ancient tree that would help him reconnect with the roots of hearth and home.

Trees such as these oaks grow very slowly and are long-lived. Jensen pointed out that if given the proper respect, the tree would live another century or more. Prairie oaks such as those remaining at Fair Lane remind us of another age, before the prairie fires were quenched and these lone scattered monarchs spread wide their branches while in open prairie filled with flowers. Cadillac wrote of these oaks in his journals. To Jensen, they were God's benchmarks, left for us as reminders of the Divine's role in shaping this land that now is our home. According to Jensen, Ford should have counted himself blessed to have so many of these 200- and 300-year-old trees.

Jensen was part teacher and part Nordic nature priest, a personage whose passion Ford appreciated. Fair Lane was the first of many Ford signature buildings landscaped by Jensen: four homes for Edsel, the Dearborn Inn, Henry Ford Hospital, and the Henry Ford Museum and Village drive entrance and the Rotunda. Jensen sometimes sounded more like a preacher than a landscape man, but Ford conceded, "If the oak means that much to you, I will leave it stand." Ford presumably heard the sermon of the tree every day until he died.

In another scenario at Fair Lane, Ford granted an interview to Ethylyn T. Clough of *Michigan Women* magazine in the late winter or early spring of 1926. The sunporch of Fair Lane was the most likely loca-

The sunporch, the most "lived-in" room of the Estate, offered a splendid view of the Rouge River. At the bend of the river, Henry Ford looked upstream and down and liked what he saw—the formerly rare wood ducks and heron were becoming common again. These birds are a joy to see and a beauty Ford helped to pass on by pushing through legislation to save the birds. (Photograph from the Collections of the Henry Ford Estate. Manning Bros. Collection)

tion for a private audience with Ford because the Fords enjoyed the birds at the feeder the riverscape year round, and thus the songs and activities of the birds could share the focus. Clara Ford was on the magazine committee and thus made possible the interview that resulted in a lengthy article descriptive of life at Fair Lane. The article was published in May and was entitled "Spring on the Estate." Sources for the article included the 1913 Ornithological Survey, Michigan Audubon Society Board records, references of the period, and current observations of the bird life at Fair Lane.

The sunporch is where the Fords lived next to the birds and is a special place. As much as Ford sometimes rued the size and cost of the residence, the grounds, the birds, and the intimacy with nature are what gave Fair Lane special meaning to both Henry and Clara.

In the interview, Ford acknowledged to Ethylyn that in wet summers, there was a mosquito problem along the river. However, he said he had two shifts working to keep them under control—the birds by day, and the bats by night. He was especially proud of his "bat-eries."

Hundreds of varieties of birds still can be seen at Fair Lane. Herons—three different species—are common sights, including the black-crowned night heron by the dam, green heron, and the great blues. Also common are ducks, including the wood duck that was on the verge of extinction until the Weeks-McLean Migratory Bird Act (which Ford helped to have passed) gave the birds the helping hand they needed and deserved. The naturalist John Burroughs said he saw more birds at Fair Lane in one day than he had seen at any other site he had visited. The ornithologists who did a report on the grounds found that well over 200 species frequented the grounds. Some had seen more than 100 species of birds in one day alone. Ford treated the birds exceptionally well. There were 500 birdhouses on Fair Lane, plus many feeding stations and birdbaths, some of them heated.

When Ford was on the board of directors of the Michigan Audubon Society (circa 1913, when the Weeks-McLean Migratory Bird Bill was up for final consideration by Congress), he had a special study done of the entire grounds, and then proceeded to implement its recommendations wherever it seemed prudent. In Ethylyn's article, Ford told the story of one Easter Sunday, after a heavy snowstorm. That day, Henry and Clara had noticed birds circling one of the feeding stations across the river from the sunroom. A glass showed there was no food for the birds. Because it was inconvenient to reach, Ford called an employee on the other side of the river and delegated him to carry food to the shelter. Later, tracks across the snow and the busy contentment of birds showed the service had been rendered. Ford's theory was that if birds were provided for during the scarcity of winter, they would never leave and their songs would cheer the Fords

The dam at Fair Lane was waterscaped into a dam of beauty by Jens Jensen, the landscape artist of the Fords.

year 'round. That is why Ford equipped the bird fountain at Burroughs' grotto with a steam pipe bent around it to keep it clear of ice. Such a naturalist as John Burroughs, Ford must have felt, should be serenaded daily. Burroughs' nickname was John-of-birds. John-of-mountains (John Muir) and his Sierra Club may be fine for those who live in the Western states, but John-of-birds had a message more people should follow, allowing them to enjoy their backyards as Ford did.

The Lure of the Land: A Walk with Henry Ford

There are times when the interpretation of any historic site seems to assume a life of its own. The spirit of the moment catches one interpreter, and it is passed to others and soon becomes gospel. Such perhaps is the folklore surrounding Henry Ford's "favorite" walk at Fair Lane. We do not know for sure if such a walk existed.

An English friend once told me to "always take the same path." In so doing, we can note the changes each new day brings as we become witness to the ever-changing continuity of the seasons of the year and of life. Ford took a more rambling approach to his enjoyment of nature. I estimate that he would fall more on the activist side of the passivist/activist nature lover controversy that kept many outdoor clubs in full debate during the early twentieth century. That debate has ended only in the sense that the activists have discovered snowmobiles, jet skis, dirt bikes, and ATVs which, for the most part, have peeled them away from those who like to enjoy nature with the "quiet eye" of John Burroughs. However, even John Burroughs was lured into becoming a more activist nature lover, if film and story are to be believed. First, there is film footage of Henry and John target shooting by the Sugar House, which is a half-mile walk through the woods to the north of the residence. There is also footage of John exercising the Model T that Henry had given him to demonstrate how the car enabled one to enjoy more of nature.

The image that sticks in my mind is from all the stories of Henry Ford slipping down the back servant's stairs of the residence to go outdoors and chop wood. According to the journals remaining from the famous camping trips of the Four Vagabonds (Henry Ford, John Burroughs, Thomas Edison, and Harvey Firestone, who used to go camping together every summer), chopping wood also was one of Henry Ford's favorite activities in camp. Ford purposely had trees left in place for months on end for him to chop. Perhaps it was reliving a childhood memory of chopping wood for his beloved mother, Mary Litogot Ford, that made this farm chore so attractive to Ford. Perhaps it was the insight that every chop of wood reveals or promises to reveal. In any case, walking with an ax slung over one's shoulder does not lend itself well to casual birding or nature observation. An ax is heavy and is meant for chopping. Thus, the axman seeks release of tension by splitting wood for the fire. In one of Ford's favorite rooms at Fair Lane is the quotation, taken from Thoreau and beautifully carved into the mantelpiece in the Field Room:

This aerial view shows the Fair Lane complex. The house is in the upper portion of the photograph; the powerhouse is in the lower right corner of the photograph. The Fords located their estate at the bend in the Rouge River, with views upstream and downstream. (Photograph from the Collections of Henry Ford Museum & Greenfield Village)

"Chop your own wood, and it will warm you twice."

The woods of Fair Lane thus were a shock absorber for Henry Ford to seek relief of tensions on the one hand and inspiration on the other. Ford was the amateur naturalist whose friendships included two of the three most famous naturalists of the day: John Burroughs of New York, and Jack Miner of Canada. These friendships thrived amid activity both in nature and with nature. Ford once called his ax "my key" when he found outbuildings padlocked. Perhaps Ford's ax also was the key to his love of nature—a love based on both interaction and passive enjoyment, of splitting wood and the work well done after which his mother had said real fun could be begun.

This walk, circa 1941, follows the route on which Henry Ford took George Washington Carver, as it is remembered by Austin Curtis, who was Carver's African-American assistant. It begins at the powerhouse that Thomas Edison helped to build and ends with Clara and Henry Ford's rendition of Santa's Workshop. This was a little log cabin tucked in a corner of Ford's 7,000 acres of woods, waters, and fields, where the Fords delighted children at Christmas from 1908 to 1950.

The first place to which Henry Ford took visitors was his powerhouse. The lovely but massive stone path first passed the boilers and the wheel room with its 1.5-ton flywheels. Thomas Edison had been gone for a decade, but to Ford at this time, Edison's spirit lived on and his cornerstone was still there to tell its story. The cornerstone was just down the steps to the right. To the left, the river rolled on in the same way that it did in 1914 at the laying of the cornerstone. You would hardly know that a working dam is located under such a beautiful veil of water. Ford enjoyed all the waterfalls and springs of the Upper Peninsula, but the natives of the Upper Peninsula would never believe one of the most beautiful waterfalls in the state was in Dearborn, created by landscape artist Jens Jensen in partnership with God and with Henry Ford's money.

The next stop on Ford's hike was his memorial to a man of letters and nature, John Burroughs. By 1941, Burroughs had been gone two decades, but his spirit lived on in the song of the birds that frequented the birdbath and grotto dedicated by Ford to his honor. The ledgerock of the grotto differed from that used elsewhere in the Estate. It was brought there from upstate New York. They were the stones that John Burroughs dragged from fields when he was a boy to clear the field for the planter and to make stone fences. From their number, it is easy to see why so many New York farmers moved from stony New England to Michigan as soon as the Indians were were driven off the land.

John Burroughs' signature on the rock behind the statue probably was pointed out by Ford to visitors. On that day in 1918 when they dedicated the grotto, Burroughs personally inscribed the rock and laid it together with Ford's stone—the one with "HF" on it.

Next, according to Curtis' memory, Ford probably took Carver and Curtis to the two-story earth-integrated boathouse. Few people have seen a boathouse such as this one. Film of Clara gives the appearance that Clara is driving her boat into the side of a cliff. Jensen was a master of stonework. Thus, it is no wonder that Edsel hired Jensen to landscape four of his homes, including Gaukler Point.

The *Callie B.* was an electric boat used by the Fords on the Rouge River upstream of the dam. It may not have been much for speed, but it would get you there and back. It was quieter than a canoe, allowing its passengers to silently invade the domain of the wildlife— ducks, deer, and birds.

Next, Ford took Carver and Curtis to two of his favorite places on the Estate: the skating pond and Santa's Workshop. Perhaps Ford thought his Southern guests might appreciate reminders of ice and snow. They walked down the long meadow, which Jensen had labeled the "path of the setting sun in summer." Ford probably called it simply a nice place to take a walk.

At first, Ford probably thought this large meadow was a huge waste of space. However, when Jensen said that people would need such spaces to "think big thoughts," perhaps Ford paused to drink the beauty of the place. Ford once had a golf tee placed there, but he thought golf was a waste of time for which he did not have the patience and eventually it was removed.

At the end of the meadow is a skating house, and although it was summer at the time of this walk, Carver and Curtis probably could imagine what a delight it was to skate among such pleasant surroundings, with the birch trees catching the afternoon light across the pond. Ford loved skating so much that on one occasion when there was a moonless night and he wanted to skate, he lined up Model Ts around the edge of the pond and used their headlight beams to light the pond so he could skate. Being from the South, Carver and Curtis may not have appreciated what a sense of freedom and what good exercise skating was for northerners such as Ford.

On this walk, Ford and his two guests soon arrived at Santa's Workshop in the middle of the woods. Ford believed that nothing could compare with the smiles and laughter of dozens of children. He enjoyed Christmas more than any other holiday, and particularly a new-fallen snow which would lay an emerald and white blanket that made everything sparkle. Ford never went to Richmond Hill until late February or March. It was the mud of early spring that caused him to leave. To Ford, ice and snow meant play and sparkling memories of the past or those yet to be made. On a snowy day, the 1900 Portland Cutter parked in Ford's garage would have made for a quick ride for the party back to the residence. Thus concluded the walk.

Henry Ford loved ice skating almost as much as he loved dancing. According to folklore, on one dark night, Henry Ford rode down the meadow to his ice skating pond with a number of Model Ts and used their headlights to provide artificial moonlight. As Ford's garage had extra bicycles, so did his skating lodge on the west side of the pond have extra ice skates for everyone to join the winter fun that Ford cherished, whether in a sleigh or on flashing blades. (Left) This was the skating warming house at Fair Lane pond. (Right) Henry Ford, the ice skater. (Photographs from the Collections of Henry Ford Museum & Greenfield Village)

To Ford, another jewel of his northern snow-filled life was his Santa's Workshop. Henry and Clara Ford started Santa's Workshop in 1908 as a magical interpretation of the modern Santa Claus, and it was in full swing by 1916. Each year, dozens of children visited the workshop to see Santa Claus, to select a gift from his workshop, and to warm themselves with a bowl of hot soup. It was a half-mile walk, but Ford servicemen were always nearby and ready to provide a ride.

Perhaps Ford also took Carver and Curtis through some of his soybean fields or to look for some promising weeds for the new laboratory to investigate. In Ford's perspective, the definition that a weed is merely a plant in the wrong place is only half right. Ford wanted to be able to determine the potential of each plant for beneficial use.

Henry Ford was as proud of his work with plants as he was of his work with cars. He also was a patron of agricultural schools for a long time, especially schools that served poor rural whites or blacks. Most often, this took place by way of donations of tractors, but Henry also put cash on the line when it came to schools he felt were particularly deserving. His first cash donation to Tuskegee Institute as recorded in the Ford archives was made in 1911.

According to park service personnel who now interpret the life of Booker T. Washington, president of Tuskegee Institute at the time, Washington was about to travel to Detroit to meet with Henry Ford when he had to change plans due to his health. Tuskegee Institute's successor in fame at that time was the great agricultural botanist, Dr. George Washington Carver. Over the years, Ford and Carver became intimate friends. Austin Curtis, Carver's key assistant who accompanied Dr. Carver on his visit to Fair Lane, joined Dr. Richard

Wright, founder of the Detroit African-American Museum, along with Fair Lane and Henry Ford museum staff for an extended lunch one day in Fair Lane's library.

The following historical vignette of the visit of Dr. George Washington Carver and the Carver Laboratory dedication, on the sunporch at Fair Lane, is based on three accounts: (1) Austin Curtis' remarks; (2) the firsthand account by an old neighbor, Irv Guest, of Ford and Carver walking together through the soybean fields; and (3) the oral history shared by Clem Glotzhober, a Michigan State University-trained botanist who worked for Ford. Glotzhober had been assigned to Carver for the short time Carver was in residence at the Laboratory (formerly Fair Lane and Dearborn's waterworks), which in 1941 was dedicated to the honor of Dr. Carver.

Irv Guest, my Dearborn neighbor of many years, recalled seeing Ford and Carver walking through a soybean field. What surprised Irv was that they were sampling the weeds rather than the soybeans. Most people in Dearborn had a difficult time accepting soybeans as a crop, much less the weeds that grew for free and without cultivation. What is even more surprising is the assignment Ford gave regarding the dandelions growing in the then-wide median of Southfield Road. A young graduate of Michigan Agricultural College, today known as Michigan State University, Clem Glotzhober at the time carried out this dandelion project for Ford. First, Ford had Clem pick a couple of bags full of the seeds. When Ford saw how quickly Clem gathered up four more bags, he had him use a portable tank-type vacuum cleaner rigged up with a generator truck. Clem said it caused a slowdown of traffic—people were trying to determine what was going on there. Ford thought he might be able to use the light, fluffy seeds as a wartime substitute for kapok for life jackets.

George Washington Carver was a bit more practical. The dandelion was an excellent source of greens, including those weed sandwiches Ford and Carver sampled together. The sandwiches were served with wild mustard, shepherd's purse, and lamb's quarters at the dedi-

cation of the laboratory that was named in Carver's honor. Nature has secrets and new opportunities that await us for the simple asking, Carver stated. When Clem asked Carver how the scientist had unlocked the secrets of the peanut, Carver's quick reply was that "I prayed to God that I might know the peanut."

To Ford and Carver, life really was that simple—all you needed was to be prepared to enjoy and endure the consequences. Hard work was not the consequence dreaded by Ford. His old neighbors called him "Crazy Henry" and "Lying Hank" because of what he said he planned to do. Even in his Experimental Room, Ford felt it necessary to install a privacy gate and to wall off part of that beautiful aerie. He told his engineer, Eugene Farkas, that he wanted to test the wildest ideas but those ideas should be kept private before the rumor mill started. It probably started when Ford began dandelion harvesting, but Ford felt the opportunity was worth exploring.

Over the years, Ford's reputation has suffered from an onslaught of negative biographies, movies, and film programs. Their script writers have not had sixteen years to listen to respected and independent sources who confirm not only Ford's failures but many of the early heroic attributes of Ford. In reconciling the polarity of views on Ford, whether it be his equal opportunity employment stand with his anti-Semitic publications,[3-11] a writer can draw conclusions from what his sources say. Austin Curtis, Dr. Carver's African-American assistant who sat in on many meetings of Ford and Carver at Fair Lane, at Tuskegee Institute, at Ford's Georgia retreat, and the enterprise at Richmond Hill, was both adamant and persistent in his view that Ford did not have a racist bone in his body.

Clem Glotzhober spoke with respect and admiration for a Ford who kept trying to push back the walls of ignorance when it came to our knowledge of plants, even when Ford was well into his eighth decade. Ford hardly resembles the closed and cold character of so many recent portrayals.

STONES OF FAIR LANE

Music & Lyrics by Donn P. Werling

2. Oh, I traveled from Ireland to England
   To find a view 'round the bend.
   And the charm of her castles and gardens
   Brought in focus the path to new lands.

CHAPTER FOUR

THE TUNNEL AND THE LINDBERGH GATES

The theme of David Lowenthal's seminal book, *The Past Is a Foreign Country*, is that although people have tried to revisit the past using wild, sundry, and historical methodologies, the past will always remain a foreign land and interpreters will always be needed. Try as we might, using various arts and contrivances as this book also employs, we can never truly walk in the shoes of those we seek to understand. Many readers may first view this book as a hymn of praise to a man they believe is as infamous as he is famous. Henry Ford may have been destined to become one of the men of the millennium, but he was also grist for the machinations of both the evil and good that occurred during his lifetime.

One of the specters of evil was a pugilist who Henry Ford met at the dock of his first great public failure, the million-dollar 1915 charter of the "Peace Ship," which Ford chartered in New York and hoped to use to stop World War I. The story of how Ford was audacious and perhaps naive enough to think he could stop the forces of history—by "tilting with windmills" with his chartered ocean liner filled with peaceniks—is one that has been well recorded in other books. From my perspective, the importance of the Peace Ship debacle is the opening it created in Henry Ford's life for real evil to take root. Perhaps

1932   Ford V-8

when our attempt to do so much good results in failure, the flip side of pride can surface. Harry Bennett suddenly became the man of the hour, as the pugilist and Henry Ford's chief of security who could use his fists to keep off the crowds, the crazies, and, when failure occurred, the media.

According to Harry Bennett's biography, *We Never Called Him Henry*, all the bitterness, hatred, and meanness of which Bennett was accused by the press, labor, and many sectors of Ford's own family stemmed from Henry Ford. In his biography, Bennett even traces Ford's anti-Semitic ramblings of the 1920s to the Peace Ship and some of its Jewish participants, who accused their fellow Jews in Europe of being war profiteers and callous financial manipulators. The truth is hard to divine. Although the past remains a foreign country, human evolution proceeds slowly. Thus, interpretation of the past can perhaps shed some light on why Henry, an overnight world hero with his five-dollar-per-day wage that doubled wages and helped double Detroit's population and his car for the masses, began showing some of the dark side of his humanity in the 1920s and 1930s. How could a man, who seemed to treat everyone so humbly, rationally, and humanely on an individual basis, not only hire but direct and collaborate with a man such as Harry Bennett? Bennett seemed the antithesis of the fiddling folk hero of the five-dollars-a-day; the pioneering savior of our heritage, both the birds and historic sites; and the creator of utopias for the poorest of the poor in Georgia, Alabama, and the Upper Peninsula of Michigan. It does not seem rational, and it is not.

The oldest part of the brain in the human being that overpowers all rational thought is the base of the brain. When the brain stem triggers the "fight or flight" response, it does not argue with the rational right brain nor the intuitive left brain. The base of the brain dictates, and what it dictates is neither rational, based on empirical judgment, nor intuitive, based on some normative or moral derivative. Long before Henry Ford jumped the Peace Ship in Norway in 1915, his confidence in his endeavor to save the world from war had been eroded—first by his wife and Thomas Edison, who had refused to accompany him on the trip, and then by President Woodrow Wilson, who refused to endorse the trip. Perhaps most of all, it was the frenzy of people and press who had once lavished praise on Ford and now turned on him with mockery and invective. It is interesting to speculate which Bible passages Henry Ford was reading at that time, faithfully carrying out the one pledge he obtained from President Woodrow Wilson—that they would both read a chapter of the Bible every day.

After the lofty realization of so many of his dreams, Ford probably thought he had toughened his psyche to surmount the most hurtful remarks from his father and his fellow Detroiters, who had said that he was crazy and a liar to talk about the things he would do and was doing. The glare of the media in New York was the greatest and cruelest assault and must have deeply disturbed Henry Ford. Perhaps it was the New York citizen who delivered a cage of squirrels to join all the "nuts" on board the Peace Ship. Here, in the nation's largest city, Henry Ford was being called "Crazy Henry" again.

If one's cause is true, and certainly the common man of the nation felt the war in Europe was folly, then Ford must have wondered what caused this outpouring of mockery and vindictiveness. He and his fellow "peace at any price" shipmates were indeed crucified by the press. For all his wealth and power, Ford had to spend more than three days in the tomb, and when he emerged from seclusion, he was a changed man. The glow and the halo were gone.

One of the key principles of physics is that for every action, there is a reaction. Combine that with our knowledge of how the human brain works, and we can see that the survival of Ford's self-image as a hero of the common man was at stake, however determined Ford was to "get the boys out of the trenches by Christmas." When survival is at stake, the override of the base of the brain kicks in. Ford's choices were to fight or take flight.

Harry Bennett was extremely loyal. Ford barely had to voice a problem, and Harry was on the way to solving the problem. His no-questions-asked behavior appealed to Henry Ford; however, in the end, intemperate actions became the undoing of both men. Bennett also took full advantage of his position and was able to exercise unbridled ambition and "loans" of Ford materials for personal benefit.

In choosing Harry Bennett, Ford chose to fight. However, Ford was a complex man, and he also took flight. His first action when he returned from the Peace Ship debacle was to move into his refuge, Fair Lane. Clara's dream castle became his refuge, with a moat of the Rouge River on one side and seven-thousand acres of open farmland on the other. Ford felt secure at Fair Lane until the 1930s, when a tragedy and Harry Bennett's influence came into full play in Ford's heroic life. Then Ford's life, it seemed, bent toward a Shakespearean-like, tragic end. What he loved fell victim to the consequences of his actions to protect his family.

In 1932, Ford and other millionaires and famous people across the United States were shocked with the report that the Lindbergh baby was kidnapped. The kidnapping was viewed as a cruel tragedy for Charles and Anne Lindbergh, played out on a national stage. Ford and his peers everywhere looked for activity that might threaten their families.

Ford's chief of security, Harry Bennett, scoured his contacts and took steps to tighten security at Fair Lane. An old jail gate was installed in the tunnel between the powerhouse and the residence. This jail gate that fomerly kept criminals confined now kept criminals away.

Ford and Bennett knew that "to deal with a rat, you must think like a rat. They asked themselves, "How would a rat sneak into the residence?" Of course, the answer was "Through the 300-foot underground tunnel." Therefore, where the tunnel bends to go into the residence, the cell gate was installed to keep the rats at bay. Security would be alerted when the powerhouse man detected any intruder, and Bennett's men would catch the intruder penned up against the cell gate. It would be similar to shooting rats in a one-lane bowling alley—except, of course, that the kidnapper would never get to the bowling alley where the Ford grandchildren might be playing. Harry Bennett was never a favorite of anyone in the Ford family except Henry, but the record of no Ford ever being kidnapped gave Bennett special leverage.

The "Lindbergh" gate in the tunnel at Fair Lane is a small part on the tour of this National Historic Landmark. However, it looms much larger as a touchstone to the shadowy figure of Harry Bennett, who not only rose to rival but sometimes dominate Henry's only son Edsel. Bennett used his position as chief of security and his ability to get or accomplish anything that Henry Ford wanted in a quick, no-nonsense manner. Bennett became the strong-arm of iron Henry Ford had wished to make of his son Edsel. Clara Ford might have said at one time, in exasperation, "Who is this Harry Bennett, anyway?" Bennett was the man who slept with the gun in the room next to Henry Ford's room at the bungalow on Lake Superior, and whose office was in the basement of the Administration building. Bennett liked to exercise power, both subtly and brutally, and he "robbed" Ford of building materials to construct not only his primary residence, but second and third homes in the manner of the pugilist and exhibitionist that he was. He kept lions and elaborate escape routes for himself and friends, some of whom were connected to the underworld.

Harry Bennett lived by the base of his brain. He served Ford well, and none of the Ford family was kidnapped. However, in a sense, Harry Bennett, arriving when he did and becoming who he was, kidnapped part of Henry Ford's soul. Henry and Harry became soul mates in their view of their fellow humans, and the image and reality of Henry Ford were ground with pathos—the evil of two world wars, the rise of Communism, and the Depression that spawned hopelessness and crime. The changing countenance on Ford's face says it all, including the one side that is all smiles and goodness, faced off with the look of evil on the other. Ford never lost his idealism, but the world took its toll on his human frailties.

In the chapters that follow, this book will visit hearthsides other than those of the main Ford residence. In some, only the walls and cornerstones remain to speak. Others provide elegant echoes of conversations with this complex man from Dearborn.

The following popular songs were selected as favorites of Henry Ford by John Weeks in a letter to me dated June 20, 1986. From 1929 until approximately 1940, Mr. Weeks was the "director of music" at the Martha Mary Chapel, and his wife Catherine also had been a student at the Village schools.

- Oh, Susanna
- My Old Kentucky Home
- Old Black Joe
- Old Folks at Home
- Old Dog Tray
- Drink to Me Only With Thine Eyes
- Home Sweet Home
- Flow Gently Sweet Afton
- My Bonnie
- I'll Take You Home Again, Kathleen*
- Annie Laurie
- Believe Me If All Those Endearing Young Charms
- On the Cheerful Village Green
- The Lark Is Up to Meet the Sun
- Prayer (to the tune of "Little Joe")
- The Little Brown Church in the Vale

*This song was remembered by Mr. Weeks to have been Mr. Ford's favorite.

CHAPTER FIVE

THE UPPER PENINSULA AND THE HURON MOUNTAIN CLUB

In the 1930s, Henry Ford would visit his Pequaming School and mill while vacationing at the Huron Mountain Club every August. From 1916 to 1925, the Pequaming School structure had been Ford's "bungalow" retreat prior to the structure being converted to the school. In this historical vignette, Ford docked at the harbor where the sawmill is located, talked with the supervisor, and then proceeded to the school, where he would spend the afternoon dancing with the students and inspecting the operation of the school.

"Inspections" is perhaps an inaccurate word to describe Ford's visits. A professor at the University of Michigan, Russ Wilson, once worked as a top official in the Dearborn Public Schools when Henry Ford would periodically visit—not to criticize but to ask what was needed to help with educating the students. Russ said it was a pleasant but challenging dilemma, because Ford would quickly deliver anything for which he was asked. An educator could never hide behind any excuses of "if we only had these."

1925	Admitted to Huron Mt. Club
	Began acquiring Georgia land
1926	Ford Tri-motor
1927	Model A introduced; Model T discontinued

Even in summer, Lake Superior can be capricious. A rising wind was always of concern when Ford sailed into Keewenaw Bay. Nevertheless, Lake Superior does not whip up or become rough in the same way as do the much more shallow Lake St. Clair or Lake Erie.

Sometimes Ford would stay the evening at the Pequaming bungalow to avoid bucking the waves on the return to the club. An eagle scooping up a trout by a cliff was not an uncommon sight. If Ford could have ridden the wings of an eagle, the trip between the Huron Mountain Club and Pequaming would have been half as long. However, the boat ride past the Huron Islands provided wonderful sights to behold. If Ford had lived his life as a lighthouse keeper, similar to his Uncle Barney Litogot, this summer bird paradise would have been a good station. The bird life and the setting were and are truly magnificent.

Point Abbaye would have provided lee for the second half of the trip. Soon the water tower of Pequaming, Ford's lighthouse, would come into view. Emblazoned with the Ford script, the Ford logo appears almost as good today as when it was painted decades ago. Like a lighthouse to sailors, that Ford script is a welcome and familiar sight for drivers all over the world now.

Arriving at the dock at Pequaming, boatloads of logs once were stockpiled for the sawmill. Ford had dreamed of a sustainable yield, but the trees did not grow as fast as he had hoped. His 12-inch minimum diameter size and hundreds of thousands of acres yielded to the demands of World War II, and Ford's forests were stripped and the sawmills silenced.

The bungalow at Pequaming was purchased by Henry Ford as a retreat in 1916. Later, he made it into part of his school at his Pequaming, Michigan, community centered around a large sawmill. The spacious porch was used by Ford for dancing during his summer visits. (Photograph from the Collections of Henry Ford Museum & Greenfield Village)

and proudly boast that they have returned to weaving on the loom on which they learned their chosen handicraft. Similar to Big Bay, Pequaming was centered on the lumber industry. Consequently, Henry Ford's visits to Pequaming were made to inspect both the sawmill operations and the school that he established in and around his former retreat.

Ford's pioneering work in forestry continues today by Michigan Technological University and Northern Michigan University, which ultimately received one of Ford's sawmills and acres of timber. The war years and the sheer demand for wood halted many of Ford's plans for a sustainable harvest from almost a half-million acres of timberland that he owned in the Upper Peninsula of Michigan and in Richmond Hill, Georgia. His forests were chopped down en masse to fuel the war effort. Ford's essays on wood conservation, as well as the practice within his company, set the standard of the "Three R's": reduce, reuse, and recycle. This effort made Ford an early model of ecological efficiency. Ford's specification that shipping boxes be of such size that he could reuse the wood as floor boards, and the conversion of waste lumber to everyday backyard charcoal briquettes, are two of the more famous and significant of Ford's practices. In the 1920s, the Ford recycling department returned more than a million dollars per month to the company.[5-1]

For more than a decade, Clara and Henry Ford escaped the hot, muggy days of August by retreating to the bungalow in Pequaming, located on Keewenaw Bay in the Upper Peninsula of Michigan. Henry Ford had bought the bungalow, a grand cabin, in 1916 from the Hebard family, who were lumber barons. Later, the Pequaming cabin became part of a school when Ford succeeded in his quest to join the Huron Mountain Club and built his own cabin there. The first floor of the cabin at Pequaming became a miniature version of the Henry Ford Trade School. Founded to educate the children of Ford employees at his state-of-the-art sawmill located in the town, the Pequaming School emphasized Ford's hands-on philosophy of education, a philosophy to which many are returning today. All students were required to learn how to work with their hands as well as their brains. Thus, years later, retired professors of social science fondly remember their Pequaming years

Huron Mountain Club

For Henry Ford, wealth brought with it the time and money to travel, which Ford first directed toward exploring the wonders of his home state of Michigan. Business and pleasure mixed easily and well. Raw materials for manufacturing the millions of vehicles that Ford was now producing required iron ore by the boatload and lumber by the thousands of board feet. Every Model T required more than twenty board feet alone. The math is inescapable. Ford needed trees by the square mile. Therefore, he purchased thousands of acres of prime forest land, which he managed and harvested on a sustained yield basis, setting a standard almost unmatched for its time.

As on his Fair Lane estate in Dearborn, Ford enjoyed trees for their beauty and their utility. His love of big trees and Michigan's Great Lakes' shorelines obviously led to his not-so-subtle campaign to join the Huron Mountain Club. Established in the late 1880s, the club owns thousands of acres of forest and lake land around the club west of Marquette, as well as miles of Lake Superior beachfront even today. Although Ford eschewed Michigan's "old-money" families by not building in Grosse Pointe, here he was eager to vacation, if not to mix, with them. In retrospect, Ford's campaign to become a member of the club appears almost martial. He surrounded the club with massive land purchases on several fronts, which some think proved the critical move because stopping construction of a road through club property became possible only through the cooperation of Henry Ford. In 1927, the same year that Ford threw his vote and weight behind stopping construction of the road,[5-2] the club granted membership to Ford. He then built a cabin designed by Albert Kahn, which was much grander than the one at Pequaming and included a fireplace twice the size of the first.

Some of the club members' worst fears about admitting the "new-money" tycoon into their midst soon were realized when Ford offered to build a hydroelectric plant to modernize the club. Electric lines were not brought in until 1950, after Clara Ford's death. This was perhaps testimony to the old guard's assertion that things at Huron Mountain were not going to change at the beck and call of Henry Ford. Rules were rigid. No motor boats were allowed on the inland lake—only rowboats and sailboats were permitted. Ford probably enjoyed the peace but chafed that he could not have the ease of an electric boat such as the one he had at Fair Lane.

Likewise, breakfast was served in the clubhouse only until 9:00 a.m. Several times, Henry Ford arrived there and argued with the cook's wife that he had the correct time and therefore was entitled to his hot breakfast. However, she also held firm, saying the only clock that counted was the clock at the camp and not Ford's precision timepieces.

Here is the interior of Ford's cabin at the Huron Mountain Club. From the Lake Superior side of this spacious cabin, Ford once raced his canoe to save the life of a young teacher named Onia. One year, Ford impressed his "old-money" fellow club members by having his "yacht," the Henry Ford II, *beached at the club to take Ford and all guests who dared on a short cruise on Lake Superior. The highlight of the trip was playing baseball in the cavernous, empty cargo area. (Photograph from the Collections of Henry Ford Museum & Greenfield Village)*

Henry Ford was successful in getting the club to accept the gift of two American Standard clocks, built in Chicago, Illinois. One clock hangs in the club today. Henry Ford, who built his life on the good use and accurate keeping of time, likely felt some small measure of revenge over breakfasts missed.

Henry Ford probably was hungry on those mornings when he was rebuffed as being 'late' for breakfast, not because he had slept in but because he had been hiking through the virgin forest, gathering unique plants and specimens. He boxed some of these samples and sent them for identification to Clem Glotzhober at his George Washington Carver Laboratory in Dearborn. The virgin forest, with its lack of understory and clear walking, made for unfettered ramblings through a Garden of Eden, including vistas of Lake Superior, Michigan's tallest mountains, and pristine lakes. It truly is a place to think great thoughts, and while on vacation, Ford probably examined each new plant with a sense of wonder and curiosity, as well as with satisfaction in knowing he had a laboratory that would unlock its secrets.

Ford often voiced his utilitarian view of history. Whether this included natural history is not clear. His eye had been honed in part by his association with the quiet eye of his favorite nature writer, John Burroughs. We cannot help but conclude that at the Huron Mountain Club, Ford found and formed a great bond with his native Michigan. Although Ford had long envied the club and its holdings as a guest, for the seventeen years he lived and stayed as a member, he treasured it as a special retreat, sheltered from the glare of the outside world.

At the same time, Ford was making his presence felt at the club by the grand size of his cabin, the clock in the clubhouse, his canoe rescue of a teacher named Onia, and, perhaps most of all, by his triumphal entry one year by his 'yacht' (as he called it), the 612-foot-long *Henry Ford II*. The vessel stuck its prow on the beach, lowering Henry Ford back in time to the days of log cabins, primeval forests, and quiet ramblings through paradise preserved.

Fred Rhydholm, author and historian of the Upper Peninsula of Michigan, had met Henry Ford several years earlier in 1938, as Mr. Ford was being escorted through the Bay Cliff Health Camp for crippled children, located in the last village before the Huron Mountain Club. At the time, Rhydholm was washing dishes and was ashamed to accept Ford's proffered hand because his own hands were cut and bleeding from broken glass. However, Ford insisted, and Rhydholm shook his hand reluctantly. Ford's gesture made a great impression on both men.

One time, Ford was attending a dance at Bay Cliff where Rhydholm was calling the dance. Some of the children could not dance because of their handicaps and chose to approach Ford with their autograph books instead. Soon everyone was in line to have the famous automaker sign their autograph books. Ford quickly directed an assistant to gather all the books for him to sign at his leisure at the club, which he did within a week.

Sometime later, when Ford visited Bay Cliff again, he found all the lights were out at the camp because the mill that provided electricity went down. Ford inquired as to when the mill would be repaired. When he was told they must wait for engineers to come from Chicago, Ford, who by then was well into his seventies, took off his coat, asked for volunteers, and had the mill running again in three days. Eventually, Ford bought the mill in Big Bay, closed it, and completely rebuilt it with tile walls, gravel floors, and chrome plating for the engines. The men who had been greasy and muddy also were spruced up with new clean uniforms and were proud of their shiny new mill.

Fred Rhydholm grew to know Henry Ford personally when, as a young Huron Mountain Club driver delivering ice to the cottages, Rhydholm almost ran over an elderly man who was stooped in the middle of the lane to study a plant. When the man slowly stood erect and approached the side of the car, Rhydholm realized it was Henry Ford, who proceeded to ask him if he thought he was driving too fast. When Rhydholm apologized and explained that he had never before run into anyone on the lanes that early in the morning, Ford recognized him as being the same young man he had seen at the school in Big Bay. The encounter was not a proper introduction. However, beyond that, Rhydholm remembers with some degree of consternation that the staff could never determine what caused Henry Ford to turn into such a nice man in the Upper Peninsula instead of the pariah they read about in the early 1940s media coverage of the labor strife at Ford's Rouge plant, 500 miles downstate.

Rhydholm's interactions with Ford were mostly casual, but there were occasional long discussions. One took place on the bridge by the marina, with a splendid view of Mountain Lake. Rhydholm does not remember the focus of the conversation—only that he and Henry Ford talked about many things. These two inquisitive men stood on the bridge, with a backdrop of beauty reminiscent of the famous view of Lake Louise near Banff, although smaller in scale. The Huron Mountains are some of the most beautiful spots on this earth. They are a treasure filled with tall trees, eleven Michigan "big tree" record holders, waterfalls, and traces of copper gatherers from a millennium ago. On the day we visited Rhydholm there, we saw deer, of which there were dozens. Later, we saw the tracks of at least one lonely bobcat as we skied across Mountain Lake. No wolves howled, but we did not remain on the top of the stone 'fortress' that over-hangs the lake halfway up the mountain to watch and hear the evening show. Rhydholm said the view of the lakes, forest, and other mountains makes the fortress over-look a destination spot in summer.

The Big Bay sawmill. When the supply of trees was depleted, Ford hoped to power the Big Bay sawmill with a massive hydropower plant to mold and create plastics cars. However, strokes in the last decade of Ford's life, combined with the successful family pressure for Henry Ford II to assume the presidency of the company, stopped that vision in its tracks. Superior tourism including staying at Ford's Big Bay Hotel and the Big Bay Lighthouse now gleam instead. (Photograph from the Collections of Henry Ford Museum and Greenfield Village)

As we skied, we imagined what it would be like to sail this lake in summer, as opposed to skiing across it in winter. In the summer, Henry Ford and other high-level executives gathered here to refresh themselves, to sing hymns together on Sundays as Ford liked to do, and occasionally have an old-fashioned barn dance on the tennis courts. Everyone at the club knew that Ford would always attend such dances, but he was absent on one evening. Perhaps it was because Ford was musing on the discovery of a new flower, trying to decide if he should pick it up and send it to his George Washington Carver Laboratory in Dearborn for his botanist, Clem Glotzhober, to identify and examine.

From Rhydholm's perspective, Ford's vacations were mixed with work. For example, Ford worked at discovering how much money was being spent and how it could be better spent in the future. Sometimes Ford worked for charity, as he did at Bay Cliff's summer camp for crippled children. Once, Ford worked on how to dam Mountain Falls, which the club did not allow him to do.

Henry Ford wasted no time in verifying many times the worst fears of the club members: that once admitted, he would not hesitate to try to change things. First, Ford proposed a seawall and then the hydropower plant, both of which were voted down. Next, Ford donated a set of shop tools that were first destined for the children at Bay Cliff to the club members' children, so that the children would have something constructive to do while at Huron Mountain. The club did not exactly refuse the tools; they merely decided the tools were too dangerous for children to use. The tools remain in the worker's maintenance shop today, as testimony to good intentions gone awry from one viewpoint. Ford probably felt much the same about tools as he did about people: whether large or small, all deserve at least a handshake. If you bloodied your hands in the process, either by working with tools or by insisting on shaking hands with a young dishwasher's hands, that was simply a part of life and never anything of which to be ashamed, for blood and sweat were seals of friendship and mutual respect.

Although Ford seemed to thrive at the club with its wild beauty, he was always scheming on how to make things better, even through his final years. Projects such as the big hydropower plant and the base for the dam near Big Bay still stand unfinished. Fred Rhydholm said one million dollars would be needed to rework and mold the earth as Ford did, to be ready to build this last great hydropower project for Henry Ford, the builder. It was a million dollars wasted because Ford's strokes and his old age halted the project, leaving his rejuvenation plans for Big Bay stalled and subsequently discarded by his grandson, Henry Ford II, who had taken control of the company.[5-3]

Perhaps Ford was too far ahead or too far behind the times in which he lived. He wanted electricity not only to light the homes of an Upper Peninsula darkened by both the depletion of timber and the hangover from the Great Depression, but also to power a reused sawmill, with its elegant and tall chimney, as a manufacturer of plastic car bodies. Perhaps Ford's journeys of riding his yacht, the *Henry Ford II*, and playing baseball inside its cavernous hold with his friends, the DuCharmes, and other club members the year he beached it at the club were his way of mocking the waste of all those empty miles that he wanted to fill with soybeans or soy resins to build the car of the future he envisioned for Big Bay, the Upper Peninsula, and his three-hundred fifty thousand acres. Unfortunately, Henry Ford was swimming in one of the last bays of his life.

A MOUNTAIN OF MICHIGAN

Music & lyrics by Donn P. Werling

They may be just hills, but they are moun-tains in Mich-i-gan, The for-est-ed slopes where "Su-per-i-ors" roam. They may just be hills, but they are moun-tains in Michi-gan, The place where each sum-mer Hen-ry Ford called home. He came there each sum-mer to walk 'neath tall trees, With the songs of the birds waft-ing on the breeze. Like fool hens, the grouse, that won't fly when their cheeks are puffed up, Ford loved this land we now seek. Oh they

Copyright 1997 Donn P. Werling

2. Oh they may just be trees, but they're the redwoods of Michigan — Eleven big tree records, some the biggest of all.
They may just be trees but they are the trees of our Michigan, So lean back to see them three hundred feet tall.
They may just be hills but they are mountains in Michigan -- The forested slopes where "Superior's" roam.
Ford stumbled, but rose to be a mountain of Michigan
Whose shadow left its mark all around the globe — (tag) from a mountain in Michigan.

CHAPTER SIX

CHOOSING A STONE: FT. MYERS, FLORIDA

At Thomas Edison's winter retreat in Ft. Myers, Florida, one of the most intriguing things to do is to read the names on the walkway stones of the many famous and not-so-famous visitors who Edison invited to lay a stone in his friendship walk. In 1916, Henry Ford had purchased the Mangoes, his modest four-acre Florida bungalow retreat, after the friendship between the Fords and the Edisons had blossomed.

Ford had admired Edison since his boyhood days, and Edison probably admired Ford for his ability to turn new developments into cash. Ford was quoted as saying, "His boyhood hero [Edison] became his manhood friend." What Ford did not know is that Edison himself once refused Ford's request for an autographed picture of the inventor. In later years, however, Ford had many.

Edison had his own "X engines" of futuristic failures. His iron ore concentrator had been too far ahead of its time. Furthermore, unlike Ford, who delegated and funded other more productive ventures, the iron ore concentrator had consumed too much of Edison's valuable time.

The friendship between Edison's second wife of many years and Ford's wife of a lifetime was the glue in this relationship. Clara Ford was a

1916   Bought home in Ft. Myers

devout birder and Episcopalian, and Mina Edison was a devout birder and Methodist. Both women also were much closer in age and in temperament than their famous and eccentric mates. Henry Ford went to Ft. Myers because Edison was there. The birds were a bonus.

The Edisons had begun a friendship walk and invited friends to contribute a stone walkway engraved with their names. It is interesting to speculate whether Clara or Henry Ford suggested the blank stone for themselves that is pointed out routinely by tour guides today.

Perhaps the message today is more than that the friendship of the Fords and Edisons was unique because two great men of history lived side by side. Rather, it is the uncommon nature of the beginning of that friendship. Edison helped Ford by taking time to encourage the next generation when Ford was a blank stone and unknown. Friendship blossomed not on pretense but on their shared Midwestern roots and joy of living. In later years, Ford worked to keep Edison famous by taking a firsthand part in celebration of Edison's name by relocating the laboratory where Edison invented the light bulb to Greenfield Village, with its millions of visitors. One of the memories shared by Tom Smoot, Jr., a long-time supporter of the Edison-Ford complex, which he overheard from an Edison associate, was that of Henry Ford in a three-piece suit, head in a barrel at the laboratory in Ft. Myers, retrieving original Edison light bulbs. The Ft. Myers laboratory later joined the Menlo Park laboratory at Greenfield Village, where they both still stand today.

Perhaps Ford, who always carried a list of jokes when he met Edison, thought Edison would get a chuckle from a blank stone instead of a showy piece of granite or quartz from Michigan. His instinct may have been that understatement is the choice to make in many circles. If so, Ford was right. However, the deeper message is that of Ford recognizing his friend's character in helping him with a word of encouragement. This makes Ford's choice of a stone almost artful and certainly memorable.

The Fords' Florida bungalow was located next to the winter home of Thomas and Mina Edison on McGregor Boulevard in Ft. Myers, Florida. (Photograph from the Collections of Henry Ford Museum & Greenfield Village)

UNCOMMON FRIENDS

To Jim and Ellie Newton

♩ = 120

Music & lyrics by Donn P. Werling

CHORUS:

Un-com-mon friends who ga-thered at Fort Myers
Left to the world a le-ga-cy.
The mem-o-ries still glow of friend-ships long a-go,
So let us toast to-day un-com-mon friends.

Verse:

1. Ed-i-son came first, fol-lowed by the Fords.
Young Jim-mie from Ft. My'rs helped them to host
Lind-berghs & Fi-re-stones — the best in all the world
Who in the sun and breeze re-newed their souls. Un-com-mon

2. Seldom has there been the clust'ring of a clan
   Whose fame together grew 'round the world.
   A new age dawned with them but in perspective stood —
   Their mark was not their coin, but to do good.

3. So let us pledge today that we will not forget
   That friendships can surpass the worst regrets.
   And when at our best we can meet any test
   And take our place beside uncommon friends.

CHAPTER SEVEN

RICHMOND HILL, GEORGIA: FORD'S LAST GREAT VISION

In Richmond Hill, Georgia, in the spring of 1941, Mr. Ukkelberg, supervisor of the laboratory at Richmond Hill, welcomed Henry Ford to the laboratory to present him one of the laboratory's finest achievements to date. The staff had been working with both the sweet gum and black gum tree fibers to develop a rayon that was useful for fabrics. They had not developed a car seat from the fibers yet, but they asked Henry Ford to test two pairs of socks made from the fibers of a renewable resource, the black gum tree. Ford was pleased and was quick to show off the socks. The soybean suits he had made in Dearborn had to be treated gingerly, but the socks held up fine.

Of the 20 types of trees used, the black gum fibers seemed to have more tensile strength, and young Leslie Long's work with the "weed"

1932	Ford V-8
1935	Built Richmond Hill
1937	Battle of the Overpass—U.A.W.
1939–1945	*World War II*
1940	Henry Ford II and Anne McDonnell marry
1941	First plastic car (soybeans)
	Ford signs with the U.A.W.
	Birth of Charlotte Ford, first great-grandchild
1943	Death of Edsel Ford
1947	Death of Henry Ford
1948	Edsel Ford II born to Mr. and Mrs. Henry Ford II

called ramie held even more promise. Leslie and his pretty new wife Lucy had delayed their move into their new home because of Ford's wishes. Ford had a long-standing record of helping the handicapped. The young Martin girl, who had polio, had priority and the Longs had agreed with Ford that her family had to come first. The Longs' home was still being built, and Lucy was working with the carpenters to make the best use of space in what became a lovely home.

Leslie Long believed that ramie might be a better source of fiber than the black gum fibers in the test socks. He had conducted tests on the tensile strength of ramie. Ford knew that the age of iron and steel was as limited as an ore pit. Investigations would show ramie had the tensile strength of steel when made into a plastic prototype for use in auto body construction. Ford encouraged Long as Thomas Edison once had encouraged Ford. "Young man, that's the thing! Keep at it!"[7-1]

The black gum socks pleased Henry Ford that day, not only with what the laboratory staff had accomplished and presented to him, but in the promise of more to come and the prospects of ramie to provide a renewable source of fiber that would be a cash crop for farmers and a renewable resource for industry.

Henry Ford, and especially his wife Clara, disliked invasions of their privacy. Fame and popularity is a double-edged sword. By the early 1920s, the death of John Burroughs and the fame that surrounded Henry Ford, Thomas Edison, and Harvey Firestone had ruined their

The river of Henry Ford's Georgia dreams was the great Ogeechee River, a birder's paradise. (Photograph from the Collections of Henry Ford Museum & Greenfield Village)

Black socks, plastic, and rope were made from agricultural crops grown on Ford's seventy thousand acres at Richmond Hill. These samples were collected by Dr. Leslie Long, a former Ford research laboratory employee. (Photograph from the Collections of Henry Ford Museum & Greenfield Village)

camping trips as the Four Vagabonds. These camping trips, which included two U.S. presidents, were arguably among the most publicized in history. They helped launch the RV industry of today. Thus, it is perhaps no coincidence that Henry Ford sought the same part of the world for privacy as did a contemporary target of the paparazzi, the late John F. Kennedy, Jr. In 1996, Kennedy was married on one of the sea islands south of the Georgia countryside that Ford chose as his second winter home.

Ford first began to buy land there in 1925, a little more than a decade after he sailed by that land in his yacht, the *Scialia*, with naturalist John Burroughs aboard. Burroughs had pointed out to Ford that the sea islands and river country south of Savannah had some of the best land for birding and beauty in the world. Ford's destination on this trip was Cuba, to study the birds with Burroughs and investigate the iron ore for his factories. Perhaps more important was Ford's visit to Thomas Edison, his boyhood idol who was quickly becoming his manhood friend. At that time, Edison was in residence at his winter home in Ft. Myers,

Florida. Ford purchased a classic Florida bungalow on McGregor Boulevard near Edison, and thus Ford wintered with Edison in Florida until the inventor died in 1931. The fact that Ford was already purchasing land on a large scale in Georgia in 1925 suggests that not only was he tiring of the invasion of his privacy in Ft. Myers, but he also was making plans to accommodate a future he saw unfolding.

That future included the growing popularity of Ft. Myers, which was already evident and was fulfilling Edison's prediction: "There is only one Ft. Myers, and thirty million people are sure to find out." However, that future also included Ford's desire to build on Edison's work with plants as a source of industrial raw material. The search had been inspired by the doubling of the price of rubber by the British monopoly. Although Firestone's successful establishment of Liberian rubber plantations caused him to drop from the *cause celebre*, Ford had always had much more in mind than rubber for tires. Ford could identify with the sweat and poverty he saw when he visited rural Georgia, both at Berry College and at rural Ways Station, which was later renamed in honor of Ford and his Richmond Hill home. When Ford visited the area of Savannah, Georgia, and started buying almost one hundred thousand acres of land, he was labeled by the Pembroke newspaper as being a "humble and unassuming man" who was going to rescue the long-vacant Hermitage mansion by taking it down and rebuilding it on his land.[7-2] Savannah can rightfully pride itself as being a pioneer in historic preservation in the nation. However, Ford had been preserving and restoring the 1840 Strathy Hall in the 1930s, long before Savannah's large-scale preservation efforts began in the 1940s. Unfortunately, some politically correct historic preservationists today have forgotten their own history, calling Ford a destroyer[7-3] rather than a historic preservationist. Ford was a pioneer for all the landmark nineteenth-century homes he rescued, which had languished since Sherman's march to the sea ended at Richmond Hill.

At that same time around 1935, a *Pembroke Journal* article, collected and saved in a scrapbook by Lucy Long of the Richmond Hill Historical Society, quoted from the report of a Savannah building inspector. The inspector had stated that the Hermitage mansion, before Ford moved it, was structurally unsound and unsuitable for restoration because of its industrial surroundings. Nonetheless, Ford relocated the mansion, and with the help of distinguished Savannah architect Cletus W. Bergen, transformed it into his beautiful Richmond Hill home. Ford rebuilt the Hermitage into what someday should be the centerpiece of a "Ford National Historic District," which would welcome people from all over the world to visit and learn about the Richmond Hill chapter of Henry Ford's life. Although Ford was one of the great visionary historic preservationists of all time, I often hear him labeled as much less among many Savannah preservationists because he moved and rebuilt the Hermitage, one of their most beautiful antebellum homes.[7-4] Although the Ways Station area was rice fields and timberland rather than tobacco fields [Ford abhorred cigarettes], Ford always wanted to help the farmer find new markets for his products—not only as a friend and fellow but also as a partner.

The Kilkanney plantation house dates from the 1840s and was restored by Henry Ford a century later.

Leslie Long came from the farm as a young Georgian, searching for a better way to make a living other than the farm life he and Ford both experienced in their youth. In 1938, Long was hired as a ditch digger, working to help the Ford enterprise drain the swamps of the dreaded scourge of malaria. When chided by a fellow as to how he was going to make much progress in the career of digging ditches, Long responded, "By digging a better ditch than others!"

Henry Ford would have liked the assertion, and it evidently caught the eye of the supervisors in the laboratory that was the heart and soul of Henry Ford's experiment at Ways Station. It helped young Leslie launch a distinguished career. Dr. Long, who went on to become a professor of soil science at Auburn University, recalls that the mission statement of the laboratory when he launched his career was clearly stated:

The chapel was one of seven new structures built by Ford in three states. The Community House, unique to Richmond Hill and a centerpiece in Ford's social engineering, featured dancing and domestic crafts as a unifying part of the community, not merely a sidelight.

the land grant university research programs. Unlike the land grant universities that focused on increasing production and soil conservation, Ford emphasized the demand side of the production equation by searching for new products to increase farm revenue rather than simply producing more—in turn, creating political demand for more farm subsidies. Ford was a farmer, and unlike his friend and hero, Thomas Edison, he had mastered the secrets of private enterprise as few in history have ever done. However, Ford was not a scientist.

Ford did know that the key to his vision was the laboratory, and the best key maker in the world for laboratories was his aging friend Thomas Edison. If the bloom was off the rose at Ft. Myers and Edison's march was at its end, the most logical thing for Ford to do was to hire one of Edison's "key" assistants to unlock the future. Ford wanted to create a sustainable source of wealth for rural America whose prospects, long before the fall of Wall Street in 1929, were already starting to wither. Therefore, Ford enlisted ambitious young farm boys such as Leslie Long, to put their broad shoulders to the wheel to achieve a mission that was as practical as it was visionary.

To conduct research on the conversion of agricultural products into products usable in the automotive industry.

Much more than sentiment from Ford's Dearborn farm-boy days was involved. Ford stated that the farmer was his best customer because the farmer not only purchased his cars but trucks and tractors as well. Thus, similar to his laborers on the assembly line whose wages he was able to double through the use of innovative technology, thereby enabling them to buy the products he made, Ford sought innovative technology to unlock new sources of wealth for his best customer—the farmer. Consequently, the wellspring of the ideal community that Ford was building from the malaria-ridden marshes and timberland was not to be factories with Albert Kahn-designed smokestacks. Rather, it was to be a factory of the land, plowed and fertilized by the fruits of the laboratory on a scale that rivaled and, in some ways, mimicked

Of course, Ford's vision was not shared by all, either in Detroit or in Savannah. He took great pains to work with the local, regional, and state authorities to ensure that a firm bent toward progress was steamed and formed, just as wood is bent to make fine furniture.

In 1941, the Richmond Hill Community Center by day was Henry and Clara Ford's finishing school for young ladies. At night, the center became the hub for young ladies and gentlemen and the Richmond Hill community. The evening dances and refreshments there were the highlights of the week.

One of the young girls who attended one of Ford's dances at the community house was Evelyn Sharp Phillips. Whether Ford was

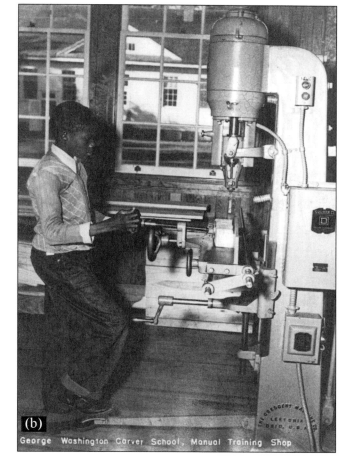

At Richmond Hill, Clara Ford built her dream house. She even had a dollhouse model built in Dearborn to try out wallpaper for her Georgian house. Henry Ford turned his energies toward creating one of the greatest social experiments in Georgia. The research laboratory was to develop products that would make industry a partner with agriculture. In race relations, separate but equal was not only created but was surpassed as both Fords worked to break the chains of poverty and ignorance. Today, Richmond Hill schools are among the finest in America. (a) Ford kindergarten. (b) Carver trade school. (Photographs circa 1940, from the Collections of Leslie and Lucy Long)

George Washington Carver School, Manual Training Shop

wearing his "black gum" socks that evening was not recorded, but Evelyn recalls "shaking like a leaf," as much because she was under the watchful eye of the dance master as it was because Mr. Ford asked her to dance. Also not recorded is whether any part of the "black gum" socks split a seam. What is well remembered by Leslie Long with great regret is that his experiments with ramie were terminated by the war and a disastrous fire in the laboratory. The plastic made in the laboratory from ramie definitely showed that it had the tensile strength of steel. Progress was being made on creating the agricultural engine of Ford's vision, so much of which had become

reality. Utopia had blossomed in a malaria-infested swamp. With the war years followed by Henry Ford's passing, that vision soon faded. Thus, the greatest hopes and prospects for both a weed named ramie and a community named Richmond Hill ended or were put on hold.

The community of Richmond Hill has been characterized as many things: a sanctuary, a scientific laboratory, and a social experiment. In many ways, it was a retreat similar to Ford's Fair Lane estate in Dearborn. Even matters of family sometimes were excluded or rarely treated. Grandchildren, such as Henry Ford II, were welcomed and given the run of the place; however, suggestions by Edsel Ford on how to improve the laboratory operations were not implemented. Edsel died before it became necessary to sell the properties. When Henry Ford II assumed control of the company from his aging grandfather, the younger Ford wasted little time in moving to concentrate power and resources back to the heart of Ford operations in Dearborn.

Henry Ford had been a friend to Richmond Hill. Perhaps he was the first Yankee in that area, since Sherman's march to the sea ended at what became Richmond Hill, to not only practice friendship but to engage the people of the region as a partner in progress. We could cynically say that Ford came among the people of the Ogeechee River at Richmond Hill and bought them. However, if you talk to those who walked, talked, and danced with Henry Ford at Richmond Hill, there is no anti-Yankee sentiment and no anti-outsider feeling that typically comes with being bought. Evelyn Sharp Phillips, whose father, a native Georgian and a trusted Ford assistant, said her father simply loved Mr. Ford. Love implies mutual respect. Ford was not only a friend but eventually a trusted partner in doing what historic preservation-

ists everywhere know is one of the most rewarding endeavors on this earth: to restore the beauty that once was, and to provide honest employment for yourself and others in the process. With Ford, we might add that he set both a new benchmark and created a lighthouse community for generations yet unborn. Ford built well. Although critics, including Ford's own grandson, Henry Ford II, are correct in stating that Richmond Hill lost money, their accounting misses the mark.

In the chapel where Sir Lancelot Brown, England's greatest landscape architect, was christened are inscribed the words:

He sought a vision of heaven.

At Richmond Hill, Henry Ford not only sought a vision of heaven on earth. Taking into judgment the many comments made by those who experienced the place, Ford achieved his vision in an uncommon way. He was not merely a friend. He was a partner in progress for white and African-Americans alike, and there was joy.

FORD'S RICHMOND HILL

To Leslie and Lucy Long

♩= 110

Music & lyrics by Donn P. Werling

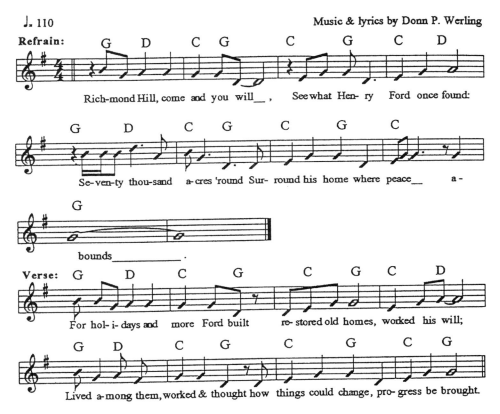

Refrain:
Rich-mond Hill, come and you will__ , See what Hen- ry Ford once found:

Se-ven-ty thou-sand a-cres 'round Sur- round his home where peace__ a-

bounds_____ .

Verse:
For hol- i- days and more Ford built re- stored old homes, worked his will;

Lived a-mong them, worked & thought how things could change, pro- gress be brought.

2. Drained the land of the scourge;
   Healed the sick, enjoyed the birds.
   Fed the turkeys, grew tung oil trees;
   Enjoyed the socks made from black gum trees.

3. Built new schools and churches too
   For black and white, fairness ruled.
   Hired the handicapped, Peg Leg Will,
   For polio's child a new home by the school.

4. Planned with the lawyers so Richmond Hill
   Would live on through his last will.
   But foiled by fate it came to an end;
   Now we must begin again.

Copyright 1997 Donn P. Werling

CHAPTER EIGHT

CHRISTMAS AT FAIR LANE

Today, Christmas at Fair Lane is celebrated by decking the halls with the help of local florists and craft groups. The elegance of the old rooms is highlighted and often magnified by their artistry and the beauty of the Christmas trimmings. The Fords did not decorate Fair Lane much for the holidays, with the exception of an umbrella stand of poinsettias in the main entrance hall, poinsettias by the dozens in the pool room waiting to be shipped as gifts, a tree for their feathered friends, and their family Christmas tree in the Field Room. However, they did make one other noteworthy exception.

The return to Dearborn from Detroit brought with it some of the simplicity of Clara and Henry Ford's late-nineteenth-century childhood. The dawn of the new century had emblazoned the Ford name around the world by 1916, when the Fords celebrated their first Christmas

1908	Model T	1925	Admitted to Huron Mt. Club
1912	First met John Burroughs		Began acquiring Georgia land
1913	Moving assembly line	1926	Ford Tri-motor
	Migratory Bird Act passed	1927	Model A introduced; Model T discontinued
1914	$5 a day wage	1929	Greenfield Village/Museum dedicated
	First met Jack Miner	*1929–1941*	*The Great Depression*
1914–1918	*World War I*	1932	Ford V-8
1915	Fair Lane completed	1935	Built Richmond Hill
	Bought the bungalow in the Upper Peninsula	1937	Battle of the Overpass—U.A.W.
1916	Bought home in Ft. Myers	*1939–1945*	*World War II*
1917	Fordson tractor	1940	Henry Ford II and Anne McDonnell marry
	Birth of Henry Ford II, the first of four grandchildren	1941	First plastic car (soybeans)
1918	Migratory Bird Treaty with Canada		Ford signs with the U.A.W.
1918–1924	"Four Vagabonds" camping trips		Birth of Charlotte Ford, first great-grandchild
1919	Ford sole owner of Ford Motor Company	1943	Death of Edsel Ford
1919–1927	X engine (The engine/car that never was)	1947	Death of Henry Ford
1921	First met Martha Berry	1948	Edsel Ford II born to Mr. and Mrs. Henry Ford II
1922	Lincoln Motor Company purchased	1950	Death of Clara Ford
1924	Built first diesel freighters on the Great Lakes		

In Santa's Workshop, located in dense woods a half-mile from Fair Lane, Henry Ford's almost magical interpretation of the modern Santa Claus made believers of even the most skeptical children. (Photograph from the Collections of Henry Ford Museum & Greenfield Village)

Why were the Santa's Workshops at Fair Lane so magical? Primarily, it is because they involved both Henry and Clara. The attention to detail, similar to the attention to detail on the Model T, made the difference. Close examination of historical photos and oral histories reveals the magic.

First, when coming to Santa's Workshop, young visitors arrived from an unusual entrance—Ford Road. Most visitors to Fair Lane were received through the gatehouse on Michigan Avenue. Second, if there were snow, the children came by bobsled; if there were no snow, then they arrived by horse-drawn wagon. Winding through the woods for almost a mile past red and green kerosene lanterns, the unraveling scene of what seemed to be miles of woods convinced many children that they were indeed about to arrive at the North Pole.

The first glimpse of Santa's Workshop was the "reindeer" and sleigh yard. Two stuffed deer were hooked to the sleigh in the foreground, while other "reindeer" chewed their cud lying down under a shelter. The two "species" of deer played off each other to create a convincing scene. The deer hooked to the sleigh certainly were deer and appeared "frozen in fear" that was caused by the commotion of a sleigh full of children. The "deer" in the background appeared slightly overweight, but they had antlers and seemed quite animated as they lay chewing their cud. Thus, the activity of the latter compensated for the lack of activity of the former that were "frozen in fear." Likewise, the former were real full-body mounts of deer, which compensated for the bovine features of the "reindeer" chewing their cud. The eye-catcher for the children was the presents loaded and ready to be delivered in the sleigh on Christmas Eve.

The second scene was the "Ho, Ho, Ho" of Santa himself, which could be heard coming from the top of the workshop. This laughter from

together in their new home at Fair Lane. An early snowfall could have meant the circa-1900 Portland Cutter was put to good use down Fair Lane Drive and the three linking meadows off the Music Room terrace. What memory does record is that Santa's Workshop, begun in 1908 when the Model T started making real money, was in full swing by 1916. Ed Bryant, one of Clara's favorite nephews, recorded his memories from the beginning to the end of those fabulous events. They truly must have been fabulous because the recollections of dozens of youngsters who attended these affairs are highly consistent. Age and the passage of decades did not dim the memories.

Santa did not give the children time to have a second, more critical look at Santa's "reindeer." As the sleigh or wagon approached the front door of the workshop, Santa would toss down scoops of candy. The children would pile out of the bobsled or wagon to help themselves to the bounty of sweets. Suddenly, Santa appeared at the front door. You might say his appearance seemed to the children almost magical and as quick as a crack of a whip because, while the children were busily gathering the candy on the ground, Santa would make use of a specially constructed chimney to make his appearance at the front door from the inside. Santa then stood at the doorway of his workshop, inviting the children inside the two-room cabin.

One room of the cabin was used to hold presents, and the other room offered hot soup to warm the children. From the expressions on the children's faces, not all were enamored of the traditional offering of oyster soup. The early years of Santa's Workshop had been more of a family affair, with parents accompanying children. When the Fords noticed that parents were pushing their children to pick the most expensive gift instead of the gift they wanted, the Fords banned parents from Santa's Workshops. Parents were permitted to rejoin their children at the fiddling and dancing that followed, which according to Ed Bryant was a grand mixture of music from the various ethnic groups that composed Ford Motor Company at that time. Ed Cushman's wife, the late Kay Cushman, who attended Santa's Workshop, was as skeptical as a child as she was when I knew her as an adult volunteer and the past president of the League of Women Voters in Michigan. However, the magic of Ford's Santa's Workshop convinced even Kay to suspend her disbelief.

That magic was a direct outgrowth of the Fords' sense of timing and interpretation. Similar to an unfolding play with linkages, counterpoints, and cleverly devised deceptions, Ford the master mechanic reveals himself as Ford the master interpreter. His later triumphs at various World's Fairs, including his triumphal Chicago World's Fair exhibit on the soybean and its centerpiece Rotunda, reflect that genius as well. Henry Ford has been inducted into perhaps more "halls of fame" than any other person: motorsports, automotive, maritime, aviation, and agriculture. To that list should someday be added the "World Interpreters' Hall of Fame," which, to my knowledge, presently does not exist.

In preserving and interpreting our heritage, whether it be Greenfield Village or Santa's Workshop at the Fair Lane estate, Ford possessed magical ways of revealing things to young and old. Perhaps that is why a young man named Walt Disney visited Greenfield Village. However, Henry Ford never created nor intended to create a land of fantasy, except perhaps on those magical evenings of Santa's Workshops long ago.

HENRY FORD & SANTA CLAUS

Music & Lyrics by Donn P. Werling

Verse:

Long a - go Mis - ter Ford ar - ranged for San - ta Claus to set up shop in Fair Lane's woods, And the child - ren from town and cous - ins all a - round would ride by sleigh to vi - sit him.

CHORUS:

How I loved to hear those sleigh bells ring ding ding as we glid - ed thru the woods to vi - sit him. Mem - 'ries of those eve - nings long a - go - o - o Still spark - le with his Ho Ho Ho!

2. An old lantern hung by the bench where Santa worked
   Glowed brightly in the wood log fire,
   And from one of many beams a large bell gleamed —
   Red and green, hung by a silver wire.

3. Cars and trucks and other toys and dolls were on the shelves
   'Round the cabin all arranged,
   And Santa took great joy in passing out a toy —
   A gold coin or a candy cane.

Copyright 1984 Donn P. Werling

CHAPTER NINE

HENRY FORD, HOME BUILDER

Dearborn is not a company town in the long view of history. Once the site of farms, then an army arsenal, and then bricktown (Dearborn once was known for its clay pits and brickmaking operations), its formal history dates back to the 1830s, more than half a century before Henry Ford triumphantly drove his 1896 quadricycle from Detroit back to his father's Dearborn farm. Both today and in his own time, the presence of Henry Ford's company is overwhelming. Sometimes this causes difference of opinion at the Dearborn Historical Society, where they often wish to talk about the French families that once lived along and named the Rouge River, a century before the Ford family immigrated. Most would rather talk about Henry Ford and company.

Almost one hundred thousand people worked at the Ford Rouge plant alone during its heyday, and the demand for housing became overwhelming. The Ford homes' historic district in west Dearborn is only one of several major housing subdivisions and developments that Henry Ford and his company created from Ford's seven thousand acres of land purchased with company profits.

What is remarkable about the subdivisions, which have been beautifully maintained by the homeowners since 1919, is not so much their coordinated and tasteful styling, central fireplaces, and convenient locations—it is how the homes were built so quickly. The perfection of the moving assembly line had many spin-offs that enriched Ford and Dearborn in different ways. In short, traditional home-building methods and timing were put aside. Instead, in a moving set of assembly teams, the foundations and basements were dug and then poured—one, two, three, right down each street or block. The first buildings were made of such quality that Ford lost money by selling them at the published price. At this time, making money was not the primary objective for these real estate developments. Rather, the goal was to provide good housing for good workers, who would not only make good neighbors to each other, but to Henry Ford, as he himself was to them.

If you take a tour of the Ford district, many of the names of this book will come to life. Benjamin Lovett, the dance master, lived with his wife on Nona Street. Wilbur Donaldson, Ford's youthful driver who took Dr. George Washington Carver and his assistant to the Dearborn Inn, lived around the block. What was more amazing to the executive from Ford of France, was that Henry Ford simply dropped by unexpectedly to say hello to the Donaldsons.[9-1] Henry did not know that the French executive was there—he was just being neighborly.

1919   Ford sole owner of Ford Motor Company

HENRY FORD BUILT MORE THAN CARS

Music & Lyrics by Donn P. Werling

1. Hen-ry Ford built ma-ny cars But of them all were three great stars____

__. The "T" was the first to be ac-claimed fol-lowed by the "A" of last__-ing

fame. But the fast-est & best in my par-lance Is the one you'd want to take

to the dance. It's the Ford V - 8 and no one could dis-

pute Its pow-er-ful en-gine un-der its hood. 2. Clyde Bar-row of bank

rob-bing in-fame Wrote a let-ter of thanks be-cause his game Of e-lu-ding po-

lice his Ford left in the dust Brought him hap-pi-ness and them__ dis-gust. It

was a feat no one fore-saw, A sing-le cast that in one draw_____

__ Gave great pow-er to the com-mon man: Free-dom to roam and rum-ble this

Copyright 1997 Donn P. Werling

CHAPTER TEN

HENRY FORD, CONSERVATIONIST

The landmark life of Henry Ford was filled with noteworthy achievements. Some of his lesser known achievements in clude those in conservation, the first of which we enjoy to this day. The next time you hear a songbird or raise your sights to a flight of geese, you might say, "Thank you, Henry Ford."

In the early 1900s, songbirds and geese were decreasing in numbers. Rapid human population increases, combined with habitat destruction and market hunting, resulted in the decimation of once seemingly inexhaustible wildlife populations.

The passage of the Weeks-McLean Migratory Bird Act in 1913, followed by the 1918 Migratory Bird Treaty with Canada, renewed the abundance of bird life on our continent. Henry Ford's role in pushing through this benchmark legislation has been documented but remains uncelebrated, partly because his other accomplishments overshadow it.

Why Henry Ford became fascinated by bird life is unknown, but his interest began at a young age. Ford's earliest memory was that of a bird and its nest. "I have always remembered the song [of the bird]," he wrote in his jot book or diary in 1913. At Ford's Highland Park factory, a birding scope was located by his office window. The land where Ford later built his home, Fair Lane, was intensively managed as a bird sanctuary, where bird feeding, birdhouses by the hundreds, and a gamekeeper held sway.

1914	$5 a day wage
	First met Jack Miner
1914–1918	*World War I*
1915	Fair Lane completed
	Bought the bungalow in the Upper Peninsula
1916	Bought home in Ft. Myers
1917	Fordson tractor
	Birth of Henry Ford II, the first of four grandchildren
1918	Migratory Bird Treaty with Canada
1918–1924	"Four Vagabonds" camping trips
1919	Ford sole owner of Ford Motor Company
1919–1927	X engine (The engine/car that never was)
1921	First met Martha Berry
1922	Lincoln Motor Company purchased
1924	Built first diesel freighters on the Great Lakes

1925	Admitted to Huron Mt. Club
	Began acquiring Georgia land
1926	Ford Tri-motor
1927	Model A introduced; Model T discontinued
1929	Greenfield Village/Museum dedicated
1929–1941	*The Great Depression*
1932	Ford V-8
1935	Built Richmond Hill
1937	Battle of the Overpass—U.A.W.
1939–1945	*World War II*
1940	Henry Ford II and Anne McDonnell marry
1941	First plastic car (soybeans)
	Ford signs with the U.A.W.
	Birth of Charlotte Ford, first great-grandchild
1943	Death of Edsel Ford

Henry Ford could be described as a savior of birds. In this photograph, he is birding with his son Edsel. (Photograph from the Collections of Henry Ford Museum & Greenfield Village)

When Ford decided to build Fair Lane along the Rouge River instead of Lake St. Clair, he hired Jens Jensen of Chicago. Jensen was to the landscape art world what Frank Lloyd Wright was to architecture. He was the first to use ecological principles in his designs. At that time, the principles of ecological succession were being discovered by his friend and associate, Henry Cowles, the pioneer ecologist from the University of Chicago. Jensen worked for six years and transformed the farmland landscape into a tapestry of meadows, a lake, ponds, waterfalls, forest, and trail gardens using thousands of native plantings, making Fair Lane one of the largest landscape contracts of the period. A grotto with a steam-heated birdbath was dedicated in honor of the

naturalist John Burroughs. Burroughs was a traveling companion with Ford, on Ford's yacht, and a guest at Fair Lane. The two men often went camping together. Their much-publicized camping trips, which included President Harding and Harvey Firestone as well, helped launch the explosion in American recreational camping. Burroughs reciprocated Ford's dedication by inscribing these words in his twenty-eight-volume set of nature writings:

> To Henry Ford, who has given a new breath of life to so many of his fellow beings.

May 22, 1915

In 1918, the year in which the Migratory Bird Treaty between the United States and Canada was signed, the treaty ending World War I also was signed. In 1915, Henry Ford had tried to stop the carnage of the war with his much-ridiculed Peace Ship, in an attempt to "get the boys out of the trenches by Christmas."

On his own continent, Ford was more successful in stopping the wasteful slaughter of "so many" other "fellow beings." This is not to imply that Henry Ford deserves all of the credit for the Migratory Bird Act or that he was an "I won't shoot" pacifist. Ford's factories played important roles in winning both world wars. In his home, Ford owned a gun collection and was an avid marksman. In his early years, he had been an active hunter. However, Ford gave up hunting when he and two of the Bryant boys shot a small game bird at the same time and blew the bird to pieces. After that, Ford never again practiced marksmanship on any living creature. Regardless, Ford's dedication to conservation for the benefit of wildlife was evident throughout his life.

Ford was a conservationist who railed against the waste of wood as well as wildlife. This led in part to the pioneer Ford production of charcoal briquettes. Initially, the charcoal was marketed to hunters and fisherman before it gained widespread acceptance by backyard

Henry Ford (center) is shown here with his naturalist mentor, John Burroughs (right), and Glen Buck (left), a lobbyist for the National Audubon Society who later worked for Ford as an advertising manager. Ford's concerted campaign to pass the 1913 Weeks-McClean Migratory Bird Act was, according to Ford, the only time he used his corporate power to pass legislation. Ford said that Congress felt that birds did not have a vote, until his seven thousand dealers responded to Ford's activism. Ford failed to get a treaty to stop the slaughter of his fellow human beings in World War I, but Burroughs in 1915 inscribed his encyclopedic-size set of nature volumes: "To Henry Ford who has given a new breath of life to so many of his other fellow beings." (Photograph from the Collections of Henry Ford Museum & Greenfield Village)

This statue of naturalist John Burroughs stands in Burroughs' grotto at Fair Lane. Note the rocks inscribed with John Burroughs' name and Henry Ford's initials. They were laid personally by Burroughs and Ford. Thomas Edison declined to attend the dedication of the grotto but sent a note proclaiming how much he valued his two friends who "...had not been caught in the meshes of merciless consumerism" and still treasured the valley and the flowers of the plain. (Photograph from the Collections of Henry Ford Museum & Greenfield Village) barbecue enthusiasts. Although Ford planted thousands of trees and saved primordial oaks on his estate, he also liked to teach his grandchildren how to fell large trees for the mill. In the Ford home movies, which are now held in the National Archives, Henry Ford is pictured with his grandchildren cutting down and towing four-foot-diameter trees. On the mantel of the fireplace in the Field Room at Fair Lane, Ford had engraved the words of Thoreau:

Chop your own wood, and it will warm you twice.

Ford also relished making maple syrup in the early spring and believed thoroughly in Emerson's essay on self-reliance. Likewise, Ford was best of friends with Jack Miner of Kingsville, Ontario, to whom he loaned his film crew to make possible Jack's continental barnstorming in schools and theater on behalf of wild geese and migratory waterfowl. In a long morning's conversation with Manly Miner, Jack's son and business manager, Manly told me that at Henry Ford's funeral, Clara commented to him:

After Edison died, Mr. Ford spent more time with your family than any other.

In the kitchen of an old white farmhouse at Jack Miner's home outside Kingsville, Ontario, Henry Ford shared many a happy breakfast during migration season. Mrs. Laona Miner would cook pancakes and Canadian bacon for Henry. Henry would arrive at the back mud room door of the humble farmhouse, accompanied by a small entourage (they usually took two cars with two people each for both safety and security reasons) that enabled Ford to avoid the clamor of crowds. Ford would be greeted by Jack.

Jack Miner was born in Ohio and was a plainspoken man of the earth. His clayworks and tile factory were his vocation. Hunting and natural things were Jack's avocation. After Thomas Edison passed away, Henry Ford came to treasure his friendship with Jack Miner all the more. Over the years, they shared many a good breakfast in Miner's farmhouse.

Jack's favorite story about Ford dated to their first encounter in 1914. Ford had read an article in the Sunday newspaper about the Jack Miner refuge, and Ford appeared at the Miner bird refuge wearing a pair of waders. Even today, it still seems strange to experience how the Miners pulled down from the sky thousands of high-flying Canadian geese to dry farmland. That must be part of the magic. Every year, the event drew larger crowds of spectators. Miner could have turned it into a three-ring circus or cashed in, but he would not stand for any exchange of money on his land. If it were the last place on earth, the refuge would be the one place that was free from moneychangers. To Jack Miner, his refuge for the birds was akin to God's temple.

Henry Ford must have agreed heartily on that point, because he gave both in-kind and cash support to further the mission of the refuge. Ford believe that knowledge, similar to the birds, should fly freely for the benefit of all.

Manly Miner, one of Jack's three adult sons, had the task of keeping the family out of the poor house with this pricing policy. The geese put on the greatest show on earth, but anyone could watch the show for free. In 1914, when Ford visited the Miners to go wading in water but instead went walking on the farm, Jack must have resembled St. Francis as the birds spiraled downward from a thousand feet to land around him. Even today, it is a moving sight that attracts both geese and humans to a most nondescript piece of flat Canadian farmland. Geese were as rare as hen's teeth then. However, to have the sky open as flight upon flight of these magnificent birds braked their wings to a stop on a small farm was a sight that seemed as if God Himself commanded it.

Furthermore, all the Miners felt as if they were divinely called. Jack simply followed the words of the Bible to give shelter to wildlife. In Jack's view, God must have given the geese a telegram. Of course, that was after four years of trials and being mocked in town about his wild goose ideas of bird migration. When the Miners drove to Kingsville in those early days, the townsfolk would honk their horns in ridicule. Ford could probably empathize with Jack, remembering that he had been called "Crazy Henry" and a few other things when he was getting started in the automobile business.

Ford gave free use of his film crews from his Windsor operations. Ford had one of the first and largest film departments. Long before Jacques Cousteau, that expertise was a vital means of spreading Miner's message. The films captured the tremendous sight that people visiting today continue to enjoy; however, they also brought out the best in Jack Miner's speaking abilities. Jack's talks were never the same. New footage enabled Miner to continually change and improve the film clips as the film crews provided new angles. It was a wonderful use of Thomas Edison's invention. The message of conservation could not be borne faster and to more people than on the wings of wild geese, flying into every major auditorium in North America, accompanied by a plaid-jacketed and plainspoken apostle.

Ford must have enjoyed the films as much as anyone. However, perhaps he wondered how Jack could speak in front of all those crowds without using any notes. That was a gift Ford did not possess. For Jack, that gift was almost as precious as the gift of reading that his Sunday school class gave to him. (His Sunday school class literally had taught him to read.) Jack had never been much of a student. He found that if you can keep children's attention, then you can keep the attention of a roomful of adults. Ford also enjoyed conversations with children. Ford's daily reading of the Bible no doubt fit well with Jack's enthusiasm for the Scriptures. He probably supported Jack's use of the birds as missionaries.

Jack put a Bible passage on a metal tag on each of his winged missionaries. He chose Gospel-oriented Bible passages because they may have been the only opportunity an Eskimo on Hudson Bay would have of hearing the good news of Christ's death for the sins of all. What Miner and Ford did together in 1918 in helping to pass the Migratory Bird Treaty between the United States and Canada was a good thing—not only for birds but for men's souls as well.

The Miners' bird-tagging operation spread the Gospel of Christ and conservation. Reports received from missionaries in the North told that the discovery of these Bible messages by the natives helped ignite a religious spark and brought about conversions to Christianity. Jack Miner's testimony in Washington on behalf of the Migratory Bird Treaty between the United States and Canada documented the migratory habits of waterfowl and the compelling need for cooperative management of the last vestiges of the great flocks if they were to be saved and brought back in numbers, as indeed they have been today.

One year, the baseball legend Ty Cobb came to the Miner farm and for the camera gently tossed a goose into the air. The way Cobb used the cleats of his shoes to instill fear in his opponents was a sight as fearsome as a flight of geese is handsome. To help Jack solve the popularity and predator problems that Miner's refuge and speaking success had caused, Ford had a fenced delivered to set up around the refuge. Having loaned Miner his Windsor film crew, Ford helped make Jack Miner a household name and the first internationally celebrated host and narrator of wildlife cinematography.

Ford used his friendship with Thomas Edison and the power of his own extensive dealer network to apply pressure to Congress to break the log jam holding up passage of the 1913 Weeks-McLean Migratory Bird Act, the legislation that led to the 1918 Migratory Bird Treaty. Using data from his goose tagging efforts that documented the international migratory habits of geese and ducks, Jack Miner testified before Congress and played a key role in the passing of the treaty in 1918. Three telegrams found in the files of the Edison National Historic Site in West Orange, New Jersey, tell the tale:

Mrs. Thomas A. Edison:

I am greatly interested in the McLean migratory bill now pending in Congress. It extends federal protection to our birds. Has already passed Senate but must have all the help we can get to have the House act at this session. It is the only way to save our most useful and necessary birds from destruction. Won't you please get Mr. Edison to give an interview to some good newspaper man, urging immediate passing of this greatly needed measure, and also ask him to telegraph Speaker Clark and Congressman John W. Weeks at Washington to this end? Kindest regards to you both.

Henry Ford

Ford wisely sent his appeal to Mrs. Edison, who was an avid birder and less preoccupied than her husband. She passed the telegram to her husband with this note:

Will you take some action on this, please?

Edison's response to Ford's plea is as follows:

Henry Ford
Detroit, Michigan

I have telegraphed about bird bill as you desire. Will see about interview. Kind regards to you all.

Thomas A. Edison

The final telegram is from Glen Buck, who had been working with Ford and the Audubon Society to pass the "bird bills." The legislation had languished before Congress for two years, until Ford organized his dealer network and used his most influential friends to lobby for its passage. Buck subsequently was hired as an advertising manager by Ford. Here is Buck's telegram:

Thomas A. Edison
East Orange, New Jersey

I have the honor to report that our bird bill is now law. Passed both houses late this afternoon and has already been signed by the President. When I came last Wednesday, its chances were hopeless but succeeded in getting it attached to agriculture appropriation bill, and in spite of the purple protest of Mondel who fought one of the most vicious fights of the session against it up until tonight. We have won, thanks to you. If you don't ever see me again, you will know that I have gone straight up in the air.

Glen Buck

Fair Lane, Ford's Dearborn estate, today includes over three-hundred acres of nature preserves land and is now a National Historic Landmark. This landmark should be visited as much for its bird life and grounds as for its mansion and powerhouse. It continues to be one of the best birding spots in Michigan. On the grounds of Fair Lane remain a number of the state's largest oaks, up to four or more feet in diameter, and dating back two hundred years or more, not to mention the two hundred and twenty species of birds that have been sighted on the grounds.

SANCTUARY

Music & lyrics by Donn P. Werling

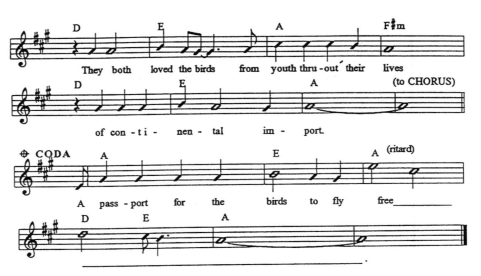

They both loved the birds from youth thru-out their lives
(to CHORUS)
of con - ti - nen - tal im - port.

CODA
A pass - port for the birds to fly free_____

2. More beauty than I've ever seen,
   Said Henry Ford to Jack,
   When the V of geese flying free
   Descended for their migration rest.

3. Nineteen eighteen, the end of wars
   Two continental slaughters stopped
   In the old world, but also in the new,
   Two treaties, but for earth a world apart.

Copyright 1993 Donn P. Werling

CHAPTER ELEVEN

HENRY FORD,
PIONEER PRESERVATIONIST

For anyone who has experienced it, the preservation, restoration, and antique-collecting virus is powerful. Henry Ford certainly caught a strong case of it in his lifetime, and its source has been attributed to various causes. In the book, *A Home for Our Heritage*,[11-1] the 1979 Edison Institute documentary about the building and growth of Greenfield Village and Henry Ford Museum, the author Geoffrey C. Upward identifies the root cause of Ford's zeal for historic preservation as one of history's most infamous quotes: "History is bunk." Henry Ford uttered this statement when he testified in his lawsuit for libel against the *Chicago Tribune*, which had called Ford the pacifist, an anarchist and other things. Ford's vengeance on the *Chicago Tribune* and the press was turned into a positive force by his becoming one of the greatest antique collectors of all time. We could

1915	Fair Lane completed
	Bought the bungalow in the Upper Peninsula
1916	Bought home in Ft. Myers
1917	Fordson tractor
	Birth of Henry Ford II, the first of four grandchildren
1918	Migratory Bird Treaty with Canada
1918–1924	"Four Vagabonds" camping trips
1919	Ford sole owner of Ford Motor Company
1919–1927	X engine (The engine/car that never was)

further qualify this statement to say confidently that Ford became the greatest collector of everyday items—what most people referred to as junk. Junk and bunk are closely related. In Henry Ford's mind, artifacts were items of education, in contrast to the standard idea that eloquence with a large repertoire of words was the sign of an educated person. Upward begins his book with the restoration of Ford's childhood farmhouse in 1919. A walk around the gardens of Fair Lane suggests that perhaps Ford's conversion to a historic preservationist was not such a "knee-jerk reaction," but a well-rooted plant that fully blossomed when time allowed, and the derogatory ink from the press surrounding the "history is bunk" affair prodded him.

The humiliation and frustration on the witness stand of the sometimes inarticulate auto king would have proved a powerful motivator for Ford to have articulated his views through the tremendously therapeutic exercise of historic preservation. However, to attribute to strictly negative forces Ford's genesis or regenesis as one of the great historic preservationists of all time is selling the man short. This is evident when you walk not only the halls and gardens of Fair Lane, but also those of the Greenfield Village, the Henry Ford Museum, the Wayside Inn of Massachusetts, the Botsford Inn of Michigan, or dozens of other sites that Ford saved for the sake of preservation and public edification. A greater force—an anthology of love for our heritage—will become evident.

Our walk through Ford's preservation halls will begin with the concrete expressions of Ford's growing passion for preservation. Then we will continue through some of the more than a dozen halls that became designated as local, state, and national landmarks long after Ford was gone. Before beginning this heritage walk, further exploration is warranted as to what motivated Ford to become one of the greatest contradictions in history—a man who would state, under oath, that history is meaningless, and then create one of the greatest historical museums in the world (based on attendance and number of artifacts). Leading up to, during, and following the tremendous birth of historical appreciation, Ford restored the oldest inn in Michigan, as well as old schoolhouses and mills almost by the dozens. Furthermore, these were not accomplished by decree; rather, they developed with active, hands-on involvement and follow-up visitation by the billionaire himself. The historic preservation virus indeed seemed strong. Its earliest source predates by five years Ford's restoration of his parents' and childhood home, and thus it predates by half a decade the *Chicago Tribune* trial and Ford's "History is bunk" testimony. It is evident—both within and outside the walls of Ford's new and final home at Fair Lane.

The fields of Henry Ford's Fair Lane were once the fields of the Ten Eyck and Black families and the Rouge River. As any river is to young farm boys, these were the sources of early explorations and adventures, no matter who owned the banks.

The setting for this vignette is farm fields and meadows along the Rouge River, the scene of Henry Ford's youth. I explored this area with my young son. Many of the scenes are largely preserved today as they were in Ford's youth. The farmhouses are gone, but the river valley remains. The area can be experienced as I did—hiking there on weekend mornings while reliving my own childhood ramblings as a farm boy in Indiana, in a region that was as rural as Dearborn in the 1870s.

The Rouge River is approximately a mile due west from Ford's boyhood farm. Sitting today on the edge of the bluff, 30 feet above the swirling waters of the Rouge River, we can still watch the wonders of the morning unfold as they did for young Henry many years ago. The site now can be reached by a one-mile hike north of Fair Lane along the banks of the river, through a wetland, and then up a rising bank of

oak and sugar maple trees. The tree roots enjoy the sandy soil while still having water available year round for their deeper roots.

Three species of heron and an occasional large osprey with a four-foot wingspan have been seen flying up the oxbow of the river. One can see upstream and downstream at the bite of the U-shaped river which today is called Kingfisher bluff. The osprey is similar to a sea eagle, and it cruises lakes and rivers as it searches for fish. Gliding effortlessly, it cants its wings to navigate the bend in the river. Heading back south along the river, the terrain bottoms out, only to rise again at the bluff where Fair Lane stands today. Ford was able to build his estate on this site of the rambles of his youth.

Downward from the 200-yard rise, past oaks and maples, the ground turns soggy. At this point, walking now turns to a dance from one fallen log to another in a zigzag path that leads through heavy bottomland woods and wetlands. After a half-mile, the land rises slightly, making for easier going and the return of large oaks and maples that need higher and drier land.

The holes drilled in the trees then and now are from a sugar bush operation where, as the Indians did long ago, people tap trees to obtain the tree sap to boil down to sugar. The pioneer farmers of the area, such as the Black family who once owned the farmland that is now the Fair Lane estate, used elderberry stems as spouts. Ford advanced to metal spikes and buckets, and today the University Natural Area staff that supervises the woods taps the trees with metal spikes and plastic bags to collect the sap. Ford's family probably bartered each spring for both the sugar and the syrup. The early farmers boiled the diluted sap into these sugary products using evaporators. Early Indians heated stones until they cracked, and then put them in birch bark vessels to boil off the water.

The native American presence was expunged from the area by President Andrew Jackson, whose administration ordered the infamous "Trail of Tears," the removal of native Americans to beyond the Mississippi. Supposedly, Indian burial mounds can be found on the other side of the river. In Henry Ford's day, the Black farmhouse would have been heralded by the pig sty. Today, the Fair Lane residence stands on or near the spot.

Farm boys such as young Henry would always be wary of one thing—the farm bull. From Henry's perspective, the world would be a lot safer and better without the need for a bull to freshen a cow [increase the flow of milk by the bull making the cow pregnant]. Bulls are not only frightening—they also can prove deadly. In later years, Ford noted in his jot book "that we must make milk out of something [other than bulls or cows]," and he did this by developing soymilk.

Today, after a hike in the woods, a cold glass of water or a drink at the Ford's mansion tastes good. In the 1870s or 1880s, Henry Ford would have obtained his refreshment from a farm well, one of which he preserved. The well still holds water by the Estate powerhouse today.

This Jens Jensen photograph of the Black farm, circa 1914, shows the location of the Black farmhouse to the right, which stands where the powerhouse is now located. Ford made the farm well a centerpiece in the garden behind the garage. A pig sty was once found where the residence on Fair Lane now stands. (Photograph from the Collection of the Archives of the Morton Arboretum, Jensen Collection)

The Ten Eyck Tavern, once located along the southern edge of the Estate, was famous for its old fireplace, around which Colonel Ten Eyck served wolf steaks in the early 1800s. There is even a short story about how Michigan was dubbed "the wolverine state." According to the tale, a guest at the tavern had downed one of the Colonel's wolf steaks and said, "Well, I guess that makes me a wolverine." No one can be certain that this is how Michigan became known as the wolverine state, but it makes a good story.

The rest of the story is still found at Fair Lane, which was built during 1913 to 1916. There, Henry and Clara Ford constructed their two monumental structures, respectively: Henry's powerhouse, and the residence. The stones from the old Ten Eyck Tavern form a wonderful fireplace in the Field Room at Fair Lane. Henry himself used to serve fireside cooking there to his favorite guests, whose bracket figures of the Four Vagabonds—Henry Ford, Harvey Firestone, Thomas Edison, and the naturalist John Burroughs—were carved in wood and hung in the four corners of the room. On the grounds, the

hand-dug well of the nineteenth-century Black farm was not filled; rather, it became the centerpiece of the bleaching yard garden (where clothes were hung out to dry) that today welcomes visitors to the powerhouse. The mid-nineteenth-century root cellar could have been considered a useless relic by Ford, who had brine-based refrigeration. Instead, the cellar received a new roof made of reinforced concrete, and electricity was installed. Guests today can enjoy the organic coolness of a root cellar. They see not only where Henry Ford kept his apples, but how he made a point of respecting and building on the past.

John McIntyre, gardener for the Fords from 1925 to 1950, recalled that Ford gave strict instructions that the apples in the left storage bin were his. That way, Ford could enjoy the nostalgic experience of retrieving an apple from a root cellar as he had done in the days of his childhood and as his ancestors had done before him. Modern refrigeration and modern cooking methods may have replaced old ways of doing things. Nonetheless, a fireplace made of stones from an old tavern, a root cellar with crisp apples, and an old farm well down which to peer into the past were as memorable to a man as living twenty years ahead of his time. Twisted or sorted, the threads Ford wove to preserve the social memory of the land belie the knee-jerk theory of Henry Ford acquiring the "preservation" religion because of a quote that is not only misunderstood to this day, but works to undermine the appreciation of Ford as one of the true pioneers in the field of historic preservation.

Ford the Innkeeper: The Botsford and Dearborn Inns of Michigan and the Wayside Inn of Massachusetts

One of the largest earthen refrigerated storage areas ever built has to be the one at the Wayside Inn in Massachusetts, which Henry Ford had built to store apples from his surrounding orchards. Today, it is an uninterpreted ruin—a one-acre, underground, bomb-shelter-like remnant of the self-sufficient enterprise Ford sought to construct to ensure the old inn and the surrounding acreage would have adequate revenue streams to keep the revitalized eighteenth-century inn of Longfellow fame thriving.

Ford had experienced what fire, neglect, and changing times could do with the old Ten Eyck Tavern in Dearborn. Two of Ford's passions—dancing and historic preservation—were rewarded with his restoration of these old inns. Ford spent millions to restore and protect them, and he spared no expense. When Grand River Avenue, the road that leads from Detroit to the state capital of Lansing, was widened [today, the road includes six lanes and a median strip], Ford moved the entire Botsford Inn back several hundred feet to keep it secure. At the Wayside Inn, he took a different tact. Spending what would be millions of dollars today, Ford built a new road on his land, to carry the main traffic from Post Road far away from the Inn. Ford then sold the road to the State of Massachusetts for one dollar. Today, the old inn remains where it has stood for almost three centuries, with much of its tranquility intact.

The Botsford Inn is located on Grand River Avenue, in what is now Farmington, Michigan. The Botsford Inn held more meaning to Henry Ford than his childhood explorations of the Ten Eyck Tavern. At the Botsford Inn and the Martindale House, Henry Ford danced with and courted Clara Bryant, his wife of 59 years. As a result, old inns must have been surrounded by a golden glow for Ford throughout his entire life.

Ford began restoration of the Botsford Inn, the oldest inn in Michigan, in 1923. The same year, it was announced that Ford purchased the eighteenth-century Wayside Inn of Longfellow fame in South Sudbury, Massachusetts. At the Wayside Inn, Ford did not only celebrate the completion of his restoration by throwing a big dance. He also had everyone dress in period costume. They joined Alice Longfellow, the poet's daughter, in what was certainly one of the early reenactments of colonial history in America. Having restored these old halls where for decades horses had brought guests by wagon, buggy, or sleigh, Ford created the Dearborn Inn in the 1930s, where people arrived and departed by the twentieth-century conveyances of cars and airplanes. However, the biggest and grandest room at the Dearborn Inn was used for dancing.

Today, all three of these beautiful inns are functioning for travelers, faithful to their traditions. From the oldest to the newest, all three have been placed on the National Registry of Historic Places by the Secretary of the Interior.

Henry Ford's role in fanning the flames of the historic restoration movement has been documented in a variety of quarters. His work in restoring buildings with a voracity for authenticity, as well as his revival and reveling in the common folk dance and music, are not as well known as they should be. Ford gave the world a car for the common man, but in many ways he also preserved and celebrated the heritage of the common man. Similar to the youth rebellions of Europe a century earlier in Germany, who created the term "folk" music, Henry Ford sought the folk fiddlers of the farms and countryside from Michigan to Maine to Tennessee.

Outside of Scandinavia, the site of the first outdoor history museum, Ford was among the first to celebrate the home of the man of common stick beginnings. Until these developments, only homes of kings and presidents had been preserved. Even the good bishop and savior of Colonial Williamsburg approached Henry Ford first, before landing a tidal wave of oil money from the Rockefellers to save and restore that keystone city of the American revolution. Only in recent times has Colonial Williamsburg embraced and interpreted its early slaveholding status, whereas Henry Ford brought slave huts from the hermitage of Savannah to Greenfield Village in the Yankee North to take their place in the story he wanted to tell through the buildings. Greenfield Village was Henry Ford's interpretation of history. Thus, no buildings there celebrate financiers or accountants. Lawyers are represented only by the Great Emancipator's courthouse, where Abraham Lincoln once practiced law.

Ford's work as a pioneer in the conscious interpretation of our heritage is even less well known. Its documentation is scattered among photographs such as those of Ford and Alice Longfellow, and film clips of Henry and Clara Ford dressed in period costumes, reliving the post-Civil War era of his childhood. Ford was ahead of his time in many things. Interpretation as a field of professionals has grown from a few hundred in the 1960s and 1970s, when the first heritage interpretation professional societies were organized, to thousands in the 1980s and 1990s. The first international professional heritage interpretation society was not formed until 1988 at a gathering in Banff, Canada. That organization has become Heritage Interpretation International.

From the start, Ford took a unique, integrative approach to his interpretations. That does not refer to his saving of slave huts and his interpretation of our nation's slaveholding past. His approach is even more fundamental than that, because long before the modern science of ecology bloomed, Ford felt that humankind and the fate of human-

Unlike many of his Michigan sites where Ford had remnants of early mills to restore and adaptively reuse as part of his Village Industries Program, the old mill at the Wayside Inn was only a memory. Thus, Ford recreated an idealized mill near the old inn of Longfellow fame. Today, the mill grinds some of the corn meal for the tasty muffins served at the inn, and it is almost a postcard-perfect backdrop. With the nearby Ford/ community-built chapel, one-room schoolhouse, and barns, it is considered by many an authentic New England scene. (Photograph from the Collections of Henry Ford Museum & Greenfield Village)

kind were inseparable from nature. National and international associations continue to struggle with the integration of cultural and natural history. From his early days, Ford admired John Burroughs and hired people such as Jens Jensen, whose work still expresses a fundamental rapprochement with nature and a humble bow to the natural world, while preserving the social memory of the land. For example, the old hand-laid stone well preserved near Ford's powerhouse expresses this

Historic film footage and this still photograph document Clara and Henry Ford liked to don historic costumes, as well as to restore old buildings. Ford even brought Alice Longfellow, a descendant of the poet, to the Wayside Inn in Massachusetts. There, Alice danced along with the Fords in an authentically restored eighteenth-century inn, wearing historic costumes and dancing to the music of colonial patriots who frequented the inn. (Photograph from the Collections of Henry Ford Museum & Greenfield Village)

who gave the same root word to both: *"oikos,"* which means "home."

Perhaps because Ford was relatively young when his mother died in childbirth, his childhood memories of home held special meaning to him: his loving and encouraging mother on the inside, and his first memory of a young mother bird on the outside. Certainly, Ford's admiration and friendship with both John Burroughs, dean of naturalists at the time, and Jens Jensen, dean of American landscape artistry, blended the disparaging elements into an expression of hope and innovation in a field that only now is coming into its own.

The exhibit at the 1934 World's Fair in Chicago possibly was Ford's greatest interpretive expression. From the press party to what the millions of visitors found interpreted for them, Henry Ford celebrated his gift of interpretation. The exhibit was celebrated not so much for its focus on cars or even tractors, but on a new agricultural crop—the soybean—and its gifts to the world during a time when virgin soil and rich ore deposits were dwindling. Ford's solution was the soybean. His seed crop was first planted around the fields of his eighteenth-century Wayside Inn. Soybeans are a legume that, until that time, had never been grown in any quantity in the United States.

integration to visitors touring the Estate. No grandly carved lions or live lions are present to express dominance. The house and the powerhouse stand tucked into the river bluff, almost bowing to this remnant of the pioneer times that Ford and Jensen preserved.

For Ford, nature and technology both were needed to work together in creating an ideal world. Ecology never opposed economics, because Ford must have intuitively known the wisdom of the ancient Greeks

Ford's exhibit at the World's Fair prompted many Midwestern farmers to plant this Oriental crop. At the press opening, soybeans were prepared seventeen different ways. The exhibit showed how soybean oil could be converted to plastics for use in cars. In the 1930s, Ford used a bushel of soybeans in the production of every car. Window knobs were made of soy resin and were used as graphic examples of how industry could replace their reliance on nonrenewable resources with a cash crop for the Depression-weary farmer. Farmers would discover that the soybean, a legume, fixed its own nitrogen from the air and thus did not require fertilizer.

Menu

OF

Dinner Served at Ford Exhibit
CENTURY OF PROGRESS

August 17, 1934

TOMATO JUICE SEASONED WITH SOY BEAN SAUCE

SALTED SOY BEANS   CELERY STUFFED WITH SOY BEAN CHEESE

PUREE OF SOY BEAN   SOY BEAN CRACKER

SOY BEAN CROQUETTES WITH TOMATO SAUCE

BUTTERED GREEN SOY BEANS

PINEAPPLE RING WITH SOY BEAN CHEESE AND SOY BEAN DRESSING

SOY BEAN BREAD WITH SOY BEAN RELISH

SOY BEAN BUSCUIT WITH SOY BEAN BUTTER

APPLE PIE (SOY BEAN CRUST)

COCOA WITH SOY BEAN MILK   SOY BEAN COFFEE

ASSORTED SOY BEAN COOKIES   SOY BEAN CAKES

ASSORTED SOY BEAN CANDY

These were the main entrees at Ford's exhibit at the Chicago World's Fair in 1934. (Photograph from the Collections of Henry Ford Museum & Greenfield Village)

For Ford, the soybean was the perfect crop. From his exhibit at the World's Fair to distributing soybean samples at tractor rallies and expositions, Ford became the foremost interpreter of the soybean. He was not a spokesman, for Henry Ford never had a way with words. He was an interpreter in the best sense of the profession, similar to those who now staff our national parks and national landmarks. According to Freeman Tilden in his seminal 1957 book, *Interpreting Our Heritage*, the chief aim of interpretation is provocation rather than instruction. In Latin, provocation means "to call forth." Henry Ford devoted much of the last decades of his life to calling farmers and industry forward to a new day—the dawn of chemurgy in which farming and industry, nature and the soil, would form a neo-Jeffersonian ideal. Such a partnership would make both agriculture and industry sustainable.

The largest gatherings at Ford's Wayside Inn were not the ministers who stayed there free as Ford invited "men of the cloth" to do. Rather, they were the annual gatherings of farmers from the prairies of Iowa to the gently rolling hills outside Boston. Certainly Ford did not comprehend all that we now recognize as the sustainable agricultural movement that is gaining momentum in the world today; however, he was on the right track. What's more, Ford was working both sides of the farming equation, creating a market for a new, more earth-friendly crop, the soybean. He accomplished this by using his intuitive and interpretive genius. Only recently have interpretation textbooks detailed the need for a variety of learning experiences, if interpretation is to be effective for all members of the audience. At the 1934 World's Fair, Ford had the press eating soybeans and looking at finished soy industrial products that were exhibited around cutaways of the moving pistons of trucks and tractors—the machines that could be used to help the farmer grow this new crop. The main exhibit building was the famous Rotunda, which resembled a giant set of gears running in harmony with the idealized nature and streets of the world that formed its landscape backdrop. Jens Jensen had designed the landscape.

Perhaps in his pursuit of new uses for the soybean, Ford came closest to achieving his goal of industry, nature, and technology working hand in hand with art—the art of both design and interpretation. Many said Henry Ford exhibited true artistry when he was on the dance floor of

The Phoenix Mill on the upper Rouge River was one of twenty mills constructed by Ford to create a neo-Jeffersonian ideal. As Ford stated, "With one foot in the soil and one foot in industry, America will be safe." (Photograph from the Collections of the Henry Ford Estate, George Ebling, Jr., photographer)

the Dearborn Inn, the Botsford Inn, the Wayside Inn, Lovett Hall at Greenfield Village, or at any of his homes. Women who danced with Ford recall his lightness of foot and artistry. However, Ford also was an artist in interpretation, because interpretation is an art that uses many other arts to convey a complex subject in simple, incisive ways. As an interpreter, Ford could marshal the finest exhibit makers, graphic artists, chefs, and landscape artists to complete his interpretive program and call a nation forward from the agony of the 1930s. It was one of Ford's finest hours, and the millions of acres of soybean fields and the labels on a thousand products—from nonlactose infant formula to breast implants from the once-spurned soybean—are testimony to his interpretive abilities. A democracy must hone these talents well if it is to create a neo-Jeffersonian ideal from an increasingly complex world as envisioned by Ford. Ford's inspiration, Emerson, had written that nature and technology could not only work together for good, but that a moral mandate would ensure they did.

Henry Ford was one of Emerson's most devoted disciples. Ford made Emerson's vision a reality, both in Ford's powerhouse at Fair Lane with its bird-shaped copper grillwork, an Emersonian blessing on the power technology below it, and in a field of soybeans, first grown to seed by Ford around a pre-Revolutionary inn. Ford's ideas, similar to those of Ezekial Howe's, the second innkeeper of the Wayside Inn and one of the rebels of 1776, were indeed revolutionary.

OLD RIVER
To the renaissance of the Rouge River

Music & lyrics by Donn P. Werling

Refrain:
Old ri - ver rolls by me, flows by me on its
way to the sea, to the sea. Old ri - ver flows thru me,
rolls thru me, makes me a part of the sea,

Verse:
Your wa- ters feed my soul, help all things to grow,
Heron squawk, or are they duck? Wings beat the dab- bling muck;
The spi- rit dwells here- in, creator of leaf and fin,

lift my bark when I ride you to
rocks line the river as it runs thru' the
babbles and sings as the wa- ters glide

see what- ev - er's 'round the bend, jour- neys that
trees. They lean and frame the view, glis- 'ning with
by. Oh what a joy of life, for in good

ne- ver end, one of life's sweet mys- ter- ries.
mor- ning dew, old ri - ver rolls bold and free.
times and strife they link us to eter- ni - ty.

CHAPTER TWELVE

HENRY FORD AT PLAY

Musical "Fires"

In 1877, Edison trapped sound on a cylinder, enabling Ford to print records by the thousands, which in turn made possible a revival of old-time music. However, before that time, local fiddlers stoked the fires that long before Hoosier hysteria was the making of a "barn burner," with dozens dancing in the great barns of the rural countryside. A violin in a symphony orchestra is one element of many that create the symphonic sound. A fiddle is a "devil's box," around which not only swirl the accompanists but also the dancers. For anyone who has never experienced the crescendo and entrancing elements of the sound of a good country fiddler, calling a violin an instrument of the devil is perhaps hard to imagine. However, for some farmers who took up the fiddle, it is not. My grandfather had his fiddle thrown from a second-story window because he played his fiddle late into the night at wedding dances and saloons and then slept through his farm chores. For Henry Ford, who was not a virtuoso but played the fiddle, it was not the work of the devil but the folk dancing that was entrancing. A

1908	Model T		1924	Built first diesel freighters on the Great Lakes
1912	First met John Burroughs		1925	Admitted to Huron Mt. Club
1913	Moving assembly line			Began acquiring Georgia land
	Migratory Bird Act passed		1926	Ford Tri-motor
1914	$5 a day wage		1927	Model A introduced; Model T discontinued
	First met Jack Miner		1929	Greenfield Village/Museum dedicated
1914–1918	World War I		1929–1941	The Great Depression
1915	Fair Lane completed		1932	Ford V-8
	Bought the bungalow in the Upper Peninsula		1935	Built Richmond Hill
1916	Bought home in Ft. Myers		1937	Battle of the Overpass—U.A.W.
1917	Fordson tractor		1939–1945	World War II
	Birth of Henry Ford II, the first of four grandchildren		1940	Henry Ford II and Anne McDonnell marry
1918	Migratory Bird Treaty with Canada		1941	First plastic car (soybeans)
1918–1924	"Four Vagabonds" camping trips			Ford signs with the U.A.W.
1919	Ford sole owner of Ford Motor Company			Birth of Charlotte Ford, first great-grandchild
1919–1927	X engine (The engine/car that never was)		1943	Death of Edsel Ford
1921	First met Martha Berry		1947	Death of Henry Ford
1922	Lincoln Motor Company purchased			

naturally gifted dancer, Ford enjoyed every opportunity to dance with his girlfriends, then with his Callie whom he met at a dance, then with pupils of his schools, and finally to watch his employees dance, whether they wanted to or not.

Growing up at that time, you had to have a fiddler and a cleared barn floor to dance. After Ford moved to town, he had to put his dancing aside while he established himself. The success of the Model N enabled Ford to build and enjoy a stylish home on Edison Avenue in Detroit. At this writing, the home is owned by Dr. Jerald and Marilyn Mitchell, who are lovingly restoring it. When touring the house, you would be surprised to find in the barn-like top

In the early years, the Field Room at Fair Lane was a site of Ford dances. However, it soon was supplanted by much larger halls, although it is one of the largest rooms at Fair Lane. The stones in the fireplace were taken from the old Ten Eyck Tavern. (Photograph from the Collections of Henry Ford Museum & Greenfield Village)

on Oakwood Avenue in Dearborn (which held an even larger dance floor) with more than engineering in mind. Ford's dance hall capacity continued to grow and expand. If there was not adequate dancing space indoors at the Mangoes in Ft. Myers, Florida, then the wide veranda would have to do. The porch at the bungalow at Pequaming in the Upper Peninsula of Michigan was even larger. The grandest and farthest from a barn was the ballroom in Lovett Hall in the new education building at his Henry Ford Museum. It seems large enough for hundreds of dancers, with a stage for musicians in the middle and a large refreshment area to the side by the stairs.

floor a dance hall large enough for three or four squares of eight dancers. The Fords lived on Edison Avenue for less than a decade, but it was the first of many dance rooms in Michigan, Florida, and Georgia that Ford either built or improvised to practice his first love.

At Fair Lane, Henry Ford II did not remember any dances in the Field Room, with its raised platform for musicians. Similar to his automobile plants that were quickly outgrown, the elder Ford quickly outgrew his dance floors. If the dance floor in the house on Edison Avenue held three squares comfortably, and the Field Room at Fair Lane held four or five, Ford built his new Albert Kahn-designed engineering building

The music and dances varied from the rough and rustic dances of Ford's rural youth to a formalization that Benjamin Lovett brought to the dances in the education building. Some felt it was colonial black tie. The dance of rural America was at its core, even if Ford started substituting a variety of folk instruments that no barn in America probably had ever hosted. Even some of the names of the instruments, such as the zymbalon, had an exotic ring.

In all of these dance halls, the one thing that did not change was the central place of the fiddler. In fact, Ford helped many fiddlers to fame by bringing them from Maine, Tennessee, and rural Grand Rapids,

Henry Ford played the violin and owned one of the great collections of the instrument; however, he never mastered playing and dancing at the same time. Ford's favorite pieces were more likely those by Stephen Foster rather than those by Wolfgang Amadeus Mozart. (Photograph from the Collections of Henry Ford Museum & Greenfield Village)

Revival of old-time dance music became a passion for Clara and Henry Ford. Benjamin Lovett, a dance master hired by Ford, trained hundreds of students and callers who took Ford recordings and books out to the hinterlands so that all would again revel in the "wholesome" dance and music of Ford's youth. Many a cartoon made fun at Henry Ford's attempts to turn back the clock. However, Ford's enthusiasm and persistence laid the groundwork for a strong tradition of folk music, for which many today are thankful. (Photograph from the Collections of Henry Ford Museum & Greenfield Village)

Michigan. They would stay at Fair Lane for up to two weeks, win various prizes, receive spurts of local and national publicity, and then hound Ford for cars and sponsorships for their own grand tours. Ford always admired a fiddler who could play and dance at the same time, a talent he never mastered. Ford's revival of old-time music included not only publication and distribution of records and fiddle contests, but also training programs for callers and teachers in the schools and his own active schedule of dances wherever he might be on business or pleasure.

At first, the press humored Ford's attempts to turn back the clock and people's musical tastes to a simpler, earlier time. Others became cynical and said he was merely trying to undermine Jewish and African American influences in modern American music. In any case, Ford's efforts have been cited in retrospect as being essential to the preservation of the genre of music that Ford unquestionably enjoyed. The *Devil's Box*, the journal of the Tennessee Folklore Society, published an article that stated, in so many words, that had it not been for Henry Ford, many of the old tunes now popular in the various folk music revivals would not have been able to be revived.

Henry Ford would be a prime candidate for an American Folk Music Hall of Fame. It is too simple a reaction by writers to discount Ford's effort to preserve, enhance, and celebrate American folk music and dance as being inspired by supposed vitriol and hatred of his fellow man. The record of Ford's love of both music and dance is abundantly clear. In many ways, the devil's box brought out the best in Ford. Thanks in large part to Ford, the music and dance he helped to preserve remain around to entrance us all.

The Playhouse and the Tree House

The Fords loved having children near them—not only at the schools they sponsored and patronized, but at their home as well. Thus, it is not surprising that the Fords had one of the nicest playhouses and screened-in sandbox houses built for their grandchildren, their young guests, their nephews, and their nieces.

If we believe a map from around 1930, the two-room playhouse once was located farther from the residence. The current location of the playhouse is where the screened-in sandbox stood. The original Ford playhouse was built for the 1924 Michigan State Fair, and one of Fair Lane's volunteer guides donated photographs of the miniature farmhouse/playhouse in full operation. The playhouse also had a miniature barn and operating miniature farm machinery, used by the Fords' grandchildren. The machinery and steam engine that operated the equipment were called HIBENJOBILL, after the Fords' four grandchildren. The playhouse is miniaturized down to its chimney bricks and to this day includes a miniature icebox, kitchen, parlor stove, furniture, and sewing machine. Even today, little children's eyes open wide with awe when they enter it. When the Fords' grandchildren and grand-nieces grew up, the playhouse and HIBENJOBILL were moved to Greenfield Village. In 1983, it was moved back to the Estate.

Ford also built a tree house that was quite a retreat in itself. It would have been a challenge for young and old to climb up to it and enjoy it. Perhaps that was as much the point as sitting in it high above the ground and listening to the birds. The former Ford workers who were interviewed for an article on the tree house said they thought the tree house was a better monument to the man who put the world on wheels than his residence. The tree house stood until Henry Ford II had the tree cut down, possibly for liability reasons.[12-1]

Brothers Benson and Henry II had some remarkable times in the country of Dearborn with their grandparents. The residence had been equipped well for children and remains so today. The exceptions are that the reconstructed treehouse is not as high, and the matched pair of black Shetland ponies towing a miniature wagon to a miniature threshing machine and steam engine, beside a miniature water wagon, are now only memories.

Rivers, Rambles, and Random Encounters

Fair Lane was a 1,300-acre tapestry touched by the genius of Jens Jensen, who knew enough to leave alone the virgin floodplain forest and scattered burr oaks of the upland savannah. Ford controlled both sides of the Rouge River for a half-mile upstream and had security posted in cars, with men and dogs that roamed the hundreds of acres of woodlands keeping out trespassers and poachers. Ford did not have any security on the river itself, perhaps because Michigan law allowed anyone to float in the river's waters, as long as they did not touch land.[12-2]

By the 1930s, the adventures of Huckleberry Finn and Tom Sawyer had inspired three generations; however, young Otto Stout was never short on inspiration. Otto's daughter worked in the Child Development Center of the University of Michigan–Dearborn, the former Ford Estate servant cottages, when Otto was inspired in 1984 to return to Fair Lane again, reliving a memorable raft trip of five decades prior to that time and remembering its consequences that guided the rest of his life.

Henry Ford wasted no time in introducing his young grandson, Henry Ford II, to the joys and challenges of life, whether it was having him light the blast furnace at the Rouge plant or playing with him high in the tree house. (Photograph from the Collections of Henry Ford Museum & Greenfield Village)

Otto and his friend had constructed a raft, and the best wilderness they knew on which to test it was Henry Ford's Fair Lane. The vessel was "tippy," made with one large galvanized water heater and an assortment of flotation devices. The boys' youthful dexterity and the slow-moving river upstream of the dam at Fair Lane kept the makeshift boat upright. When they were about to round the bend where the full vision of 'castle' Fair Lane comes into view, they were hailed by a gray-haired man on the shore.

Fifty years later, Otto recalls:

> At first, we thought we were in trouble, but then we realized he was waving us to shore and wanting to take a ride with us. We paddled over to shore, he asked permission to come aboard, which we granted, and before you knew it, the raft and all of us rolled over into the river. We made it safely to shore, but we were all soaking wet. Instead of the man being angry, he just seemed excited to be a kid again. We secured our makeshift raft, and the man chuckled at himself as he invited us in to receive a sorely needed change of clothing and to have Mrs. Ford see to our needs.

> "Mrs. Ford? Mister, are you Henry Ford?"

> We were ushered into the house, and Mrs. Ford helped us change into some dry clothes. Then she insisted we join Mr. Ford in the dining room to have some hot food to warm us.

Meeting Otto Stout gave Henry Ford a dunking in the Rouge River. However, for years after that, Ford followed his young and always

The famous Four Vagabonds consisted of (left to right) Thomas Edison, naturalist John Burroughs, Henry Ford, and Harvey Firestone. People have camped since the beginning of time; however, these four men—with their cars, tires, and fame—showed the nation how to camp in tune with the motor car. Unfortunately, their annual trips became such media circuses that they eventually were cancelled. (Photograph from the Collections of Henry Ford Museum & Greenfield Village)

also built a model of Ford's powerhouse, drawing on his expertise gained from making models for General Motors. Finally, Otto and his wife Donna, who for years portrayed Mrs. Claus, reconstructed Henry Ford's tree house—all for free and out of gratitude to the gray-haired man who years ago did not summon the guards and dogs and instead wanted to join the adventure. There are many other tales of youngsters encountering Henry Ford as he roamed the Estate. Each person confirms the experience that Otto enjoyed and treasured as a memory. Ford loved children, wherever he was.

Other features at Fair Lane reflect Ford's enjoyment with the landscapes created for him and Clara by Jens Jensen. Aside from Clara's formal gardens, the place was a wonderful setting for anyone who liked to bike, skate, and look at deer, birds, and other wildlife. Ford had wild Michigan recreated

engaging friend, offering him a treasured admission into the Ford Trade School and later a job with Ford, all of which Otto stubbornly refused. Otto did not want to commingle business with his friendship with Ford. Until he retired, Otto worked for General Motors. After retirement and now a gray-haired man himself, Otto grew a beard, built a scale model of Ford's Santa's Workshop, and then portrayed Santa Claus at the Estate's recreation of Ford's interpretation of Santa. Later, Otto

for him at his doorstep, over what had been pedestrian farmland. Both native and exotic birds were cultivated. There is no record that Ford tried to bring back the wolverine, Michigan's namesake; however, deer and river otters are seen occasionally on the Estate today, and Ford even brought a bear[12-3] there for a short time. As Ford's empire expanded and his stress level increased, he enjoyed these reminders of a simpler yet complex past all the more. A bear, a dunking in the river with two Huckleberry Finns, a perilous walk across a log bridge, crossing a stepping-stone river crossing, or skating on a picture-perfect lake brought Ford home again to the land he had roamed in his youth.

Ford allowed Clara to have her own way with the formal gardens, but he did cross with her when it came to watering the extensive lawns or meadows that Jensen laid out and planted. Ford thought nature should take its course, as it did with the trees and other wild things he enjoyed. However, Clara wanted and received sprinklers, and the lawn became a lush green carpet in the days long before golf courses ever planted hundreds of sprinkler heads, as Henry did for Clara. Some people note on Jensen's drawings that a three-hole golf course originally was planned and installed. Similar to the bear, the golf course did not last long. Golf does not relieve stress when you, as Henry Ford did, tee off and hit one of Clara's nieces. In Ft. Myers, Henry Ford became so disgusted with his golf game that he threw his clubs over the perimeter hedge. The next day, a young caddy appeared as the proud new owner of the golf clubs. Perhaps that also is why Ford would have preferred to leave the fairway in its more natural state. He would rather hike and run down the path of the setting sun, encounter a wood duck on the lake or a deer in the woods, and capture the beauty of the moment instead of the frustration of another slice into the woods. To the man who had been tutored by the quiet eye of naturalist John Burroughs, nature was more exciting and more rewarding than golf.

THE TREEHOUSE SCHOTTISCHE

Music & lyrics by Donn P. Werling

Copyright 1991 Donn P. Werling

Chorus:

Climbing up the treehouse skipping up the stairs
One should be aware.
Hold on to the handrail, watch your head
Safety's always first it's said.

v.2

Up in the treehouse high, far from phones and sighs
Ford did his hardest work.
To think and to decide with squirrels by your side
It's hard work you should never shirk.

Chorus:

v.3

His workers used to say it was far and away
A better symbol for Ford
Than the mansion he escaped, to think, to ride the wake
Of change from his life's sword.

CHAPTER THIRTEEN

SELECTED FORD-RELATED SCHOOLS AND COLLEGES

Henry Ford's Final Public Act: Planting a Tree at Berry College

The year is 1947. At Berry College, a young man stands with a shovel, ready to hand it to Henry Ford. Ford is the richest person this college student has ever heard of, and Ford's name is everywhere around the world—on cars, tractors, airplanes, boats, mills, and streets. It is also on the dormitory in which the young man's girlfriend lives at Berry College, the biggest little college in the world because it owns more than 10 acres per student, thanks to Henry Ford. Rather than giving cash gifts, Ford always preferred to give tractors or buy another farm or two each year to endow the college.

Year	Event	Year	Event
1912	First met John Burroughs	1924	Built first diesel freighters on the Great Lakes
1913	Moving assembly line	1925	Admitted to Huron Mt. Club
	Migratory Bird Act passed		Began acquiring Georgia land
1914	$5 a day wage	1926	Ford Tri-motor
	First met Jack Miner	1927	Model A introduced; Model T discontinued
1914–1918	World War I	1929	Greenfield Village/Museum dedicated
1915	Fair Lane completed	1929–1941	The Great Depression
	Bought the bungalow in the Upper Peninsula	1932	Ford V-8
1916	Bought home in Ft. Myers	1935	Built Richmond Hill
1917	Fordson tractor	1937	Battle of the Overpass—U.A.W.
	Birth of Henry Ford II, the first of four grandchildren	1939–1945	World War II
1918	Migratory Bird Treaty with Canada	1940	Henry Ford II and Anne McDonnell marry
1918–1924	"Four Vagabonds" camping trips	1941	First plastic car (soybeans)
1919	Ford sole owner of Ford Motor Company		Ford signs with the U.A.W.
1919–1927	X engine (The engine/car that never was)		Birth of Charlotte Ford, first great-grandchild
1921	First met Martha Berry	1943	Death of Edsel Ford
1922	Lincoln Motor Company purchased	1947	Death of Henry Ford

The second largest overshot waterwheel in the world was built with the help of Henry Ford to enable Berry College students to grind their own grain into flour. Ford mills in Michigan had shipped hundreds of pounds of flour annually. Ford's biggest demand as a donor was that the college must become operationally self-sufficient. Ford invested millions of dollars in Berry because he saw the thirst for a Berry education in young people such as the student who brought the pair of oxen pictured here to pay for his tuition. (Photograph from the Collections of Henry Ford Museum & Greenfield Village)

The diligent student is surprised when Ford refuses to surrender the shovel after he has dug the first spade of dirt. Responding to the young man's entreaties to allow him finish his assigned task, Ford says:

Sonny, I guess I'm not too old yet to finish a job.

Today, the tree still stands, not yet grown to full magnificence as magnolias have grown on other parts of the extensive campus. It is growing in pace with the other magnolias of the memorial magnolia *allee* at Berry College. Other plaques display the names of people important to Berry College. Henry Ford was important to the world. Why he chose Berry College, and concurrently chose Way's (Richmond Hill), Georgia, for the investment of what could well total more than one billion dollars in today's dollars, is more significant than simply a lot of zeroes. As Senator Everett Dirksen of Illinois used to say, "now we're talking real money here." Henry Ford's two grand experiments in Georgia both began on the recommendation of two of his closest mentors and friends. John Burroughs steered Ford toward the birds and beauty of what he made into Richmond Hill, and Thomas Edison and his wife Mina opened the door for Martha Berry, one of the most remarkable women the great state of Georgia ever produced.

Berry's name has been carved into stone at the state capital building in Atlanta. It is not a fitting tribute to the woman who carved her way into the callused heart of Henry Ford and who worked a miracle with Ford's money that changes the lives of young people even today. A flower clock would be a more fitting tribute, with the center of the clock showing a chicken scratching away at the dirt, looking for bugs and billionaires. To paraphrase a Henry Ford quote:

To succeed in life, you need to be like a chicken and keep scratching for every bit of progress.

Ford appears old and wizened, which is why this young man had been assigned to not only hand the spade to Ford for the ceremonial shovel full, but to then do the real job of planting this magnolia tree on the magnolia memorial row in front of the Clara Ford weaving room in the dormitory complex. This small gesture of thanks will include a bronze plaque beside the tree. It was another ceremony arranged by the successors of Martha Berry, long-time president and founder of the college, for the Fords to enjoy on their annual visit.

Martha Berry not only kept scratching as a chicken for the needs of her students; her staff had the recipe for cooking chicken the way Mr. Ford liked. The story has become legend around Berry College, and it is instructive today as we contemplate how to make our dreams a reality.

Miss Berry's "house o' dreams," built in secret as a surprise for her by her thankful students, is the setting for this 1920s "chicken-scratching" story. The house is built on a mountain with a road that is still rough and slow, even for today's four-wheel-drive vehicles. There are wonderful views of the southern Appalachian Mountains from the top, although the deer have become so plentiful the gardeners can no longer keep anything but "naked" marigolds growing—the deer delicately eat everything but the stems and flowers.

The Fords had arrived and were enjoying their stay. Their invitation to dinner in the "house o' dreams" that students had built probably was greatly anticipated, in part because its existence, which resulted from the labor of joyful students, vindicated the Fords' investment in Miss Berry and her college. Taxes on Ford's Michigan enterprises and gifts from Ford associates, such as Horace Rackham (seven million dollars), may produce the funds needed to make the University of Michigan a world-class university. However, Ford must have taken his honorary doctorate in engineering from the university in 1927 as partial repayment for all the taxes his company paid because he never gave any "real money" to the University of Michigan.

Henry Ford's final public act was planting a magnolia tree at Berry College. (Photograph from the Collections of Henry Ford Museum & Greenfield Village)

Berry College and the "Chicken-Scratching" Story

Imagine that you are Martha Berry, with your richest and most generous patron, Henry and Clara Ford, seated across the table from you in your "house o' dreams." Students may have viewed the building of this home as an expression of gratitude to you for making their dreams possible, but your view is that its purpose is the agenda for tonight's chicken dinner. Your college does not need more tractors or land, which Ford had donated during or after many previous visits. It needs cash. With the country suffering in a Depression, the man seated across from you is one of the few people in the world who can make the dreams for your school come true.

Henry Ford must have relished the fried chicken that evening. It had been prepared by the young women in the home economics program at the college. Ford asked for another piece of chicken. Perhaps the mountain air renewed his appetite.

The Fords personally requested that the quality of the Ford buildings at Berry College be upgraded from the initial architectural plans. Perhaps Ford wanted these buildings to rival or surpass the Law Quadrangle in Ann Arbor. In many ways, they do. (Photograph from the Collections of Henry Ford Museum & Greenfield Village)

Shown here at the Berry College is Martha Berry (right), beside two of her most important donors, Henry Ford (left) and Clara Ford (center). Berry's commitment to education and to her students helped her garner millions from the Fords, the Vanderbilts, and many others. Her motto was "Not to be ministered unto, but to minister." (Photograph from the Collections of Martha Berry Museum, Berry College)

As Miss Berry, you rang for the waitress and then told her,

Please bring Mr. Ford some more chicken.

Unfortunately, all of the chicken was gone. The waitress responded that there was no more. Again as Miss Berry, you commanded the waitress:

Then go down the mountain, and kill, pluck, butcher, and fry another one.

Martha Berry may have run out of chicken that night, but she knew how to keep on scratching. If it took time to run down and up the mountain to catch and then cook a chicken, it meant more time for her to plead the case that tractors and land, and chickens for that matter, make wonderful gifts, but you also need cash to buy the fuel to prepare chickens and students properly. Henry Ford had his final helping of fried chicken, but history records that he also got plucked in the process.

Tuskegee Institute

Few other schools except his own were the beneficiaries of Ford's largesse. Tuskegee Institute was one of those other schools. The earliest donation of Ford to Tuskegee on record dates to 1911. Today, Henry Ford is featured prominently at the George Washington Carver Museum of Tuskegee, Alabama, for which Ford was invited to help lay the cornerstone. Carver and Ford were sympathetic to each others' causes. Although their friendship bloomed after Edison's death, it was rooted in the Tuskegee Institute philosophy and shared many of the same virtues from Ford's perspective. The emphasis was on helping the rural poor to help themselves out of the abject poverty that so much of the South—both black and white—endured for decades after the Civil War. Both Berry College and Tuskegee Institute were schools with strong Christian fibers, maintaining that it was "to serve, not to be served," yet remaining nondenominational.

Henry Ford dedicated a laboratory next to his Estate on the main street of his native Dearborn to Dr. George Washington Carver. This photograph of Dr. Carver (center) and Henry Ford (right) was taken at the dedication ceremonies for the laboratory in 1941. The role of the laboratory was to find new uses for plants, especially "weeds" that had been ignored, similar to how Carver had found many uses for the peanut. (Photograph from the Collections of Henry Ford Museum & Greenfield Village)

A sense of mission exists to this day on both campuses, as well as a sense of proud purpose that their two charismatic founders, Martha Berry and Booker T. Washington, left as their living legacy at these remarkable institutions. Ford's own schools have not fared as well—most were disbanded upon his death. One example is the Wayside Inn school for orphans and waifs, of which forty percent of the alumni were Jewish. The Dearborn-based Henry Ford Trade School, Edison Institute, and Village Schools lasted slightly longer. The Trade School metamorphosed into Lawrence Technological University and Henry Ford Community College, which today remain among the best in their class. Recently, a new charter school has brought students back to Greenfield Village in the form of a high school—the Henry Ford Academy of Arts and Engineering. The schools near Ford's Huron Mountain retreat at Pequaming, Cherry Hill, and Richmond Hill in eastern Georgia are simply memories, although they all worked to upgrade the pedagogical arts in rural areas.

Ford could easily have chosen to ignore the children of his workers. However, there was a respect for the power that education offers, whether it was the Dearborn Public High School crowned as the "most beautiful high school in the nation," Fordson, the swimming pool at the Henry Ford Elementary School, or any of the new standards Ford set for education wherever he lived and worked. On the back of the wall, behind the life-size statue of Henry Ford that stands outside Dearborn's Henry Ford Centennial Library, Ford's words are etched:

Education is the greatest force in civilization.

Henry Ford's famous saying "If you think you can or you can't, you're right!" is echoed in the following poem by Ford's friend, Edgar Guest. Dr. George Washington Carver often used this poem to close his talks to students.

Equipment

by Edgar Guest

Figure it out for yourself, my lad,
You've all that the greatest of men have had;
Two arms, two hands, two legs, two eyes;
And a brain to use if you would be wise,
With this equipment they all began.

So start for the top and say "I can."
Look them over, the wise and great,
They take their food from a common plate
And similar knives and forks they use,
With similar laces they tie their shoes.
The world considers them brave and smart,
But you've all they had when they made their start.

You can triumph and come to skill,
You can be great if you only will.
You're well equipped for what fight you choose;

You have legs and arms and a brain to use,
And the man who has risen great deeds to do
Began his life with no more than you.

You are the handicap you must face,
You are the one who must choose your place,
You must say where you want to go,
How much you will study the truth to know;
God has equipped you for life, but He
Lets you decide what you want to be.

Courage must come from the soul within
The man must furnish the will to win,
So figure it out for yourself, my lad
You were born with all that the great have had,
With your equipment they all began,
Get hold of yourself and say "I can."

BALLAD OF MARTHA BERRY

♩. 100

Music & Lyrics by Donn P. Werling

1. She was born at Oak Hill, a wo-man of strong will, the daught-er of a Con-fe-drate gen-er-al Who had sur-vived the war and re-mem-bered those poor boys who came from the north-ern Geor-gia hills. "Come fol-low me." "Come fol-low me." On a pic-ture of Christ__ she would read. Ev-'ry morn-ing with the sun she'd say "There's work to be done." as she read those words of Christ "Come fol-low me." 2. Hen-ry

2. Henry Ford heard her call and altho he'd many walls
   To charity and higher education,
   He saw and he believed in Miss Mary's words and deeds
   And he opened up his heart and found a home.

3. For twenty years the Fords came and of their fortune they gave
   For the benefit of many a mountain child.
   He helped build a water wheel and bought up many a field
   To foster an ideal that changed lives.

4. Of her students she asked that their most important task
   Be not to be served but to minister to all.
   And the school today stands not upon her grave,
   But upon those words she hung upon her wall.

Copyright 1990 Donn P. Werling

CHAPTER FOURTEEN

MEMORIES OF MR. FORD'S PASSING

When Henry Ford died on April 7, 1947, the world had changed greatly since the time he entered it. His moving assembly line helped put America and the world on motorized wheels. His work in conservation helps us remember that we are all responsible not only for taking care of our natural resources, but ensuring that a proper balance is maintained between nature and industry. Ford's restoration of numerous historic inns and his building of the monumental Edison Institute, the largest indoor/outdoor museum complex in the world, reminds us that our history is important if we are to appreciate where we have been. Ford tried to change the world for the better as much as he could. Ford himself once said that the farther we can look back, the farther we can look ahead.

Ford's death came at a time—the first time—when the Estate's ingenious mechanical systems failed to provide electricity for any length of time. The record high flood mark of the Rouge River is still marked in the powerhouse wall. Projected outward across the land around the residence, we can picture the veritable lake that existed, lapping at the foundation stones of the residence, and flooding and rendering useless the mechanical equipment that powered the Estate with its state-of-the-art mechanical systems. Henry Ford had been unperturbed by it all, and he scoffed at suggestions they temporarily relocate to the Dearborn Inn. My ancestors lived like this every day, Ford had commented, so why should I move when in effect it enables me to relive their past?

1947   Death of Henry Ford

That afternoon, Ford had been out with his chauffeur in his 1942 Ford, visiting the graves of his forebears—where he too would be buried. He also inspected the flood and the havoc it caused. Clara and Henry Ford's chauffeur, Robert Rankin, related his memories concerning this trip on April 7, 1947. Rankin explains:

> He [Henry Ford} called me and said he wanted to go for a ride. The place was flooded at the time, and there weren't very many places you could go, but we thought we'd go around and see the floods. He usually left that very much up to me. The only thing that he said that day was about the little cemetery up on Joy Road. He wanted to stop there. Strange, that last day when we stopped at the little Joy Road cemetery. He said to me, "Rankin, this is where I'm going to be buried when I die, in among the rest of my folks here."

Rankin continues:

> On our ride that last day, we stopped at the powerhouse at the Institute. We went over to the Village to see the *Suwannee* [paddle boat]. You could only see the top of it; it was sunk. He kind of laughed about it and said, "We'll soon put it back on an even keel again." Then we went to the Rouge plant. I know that young Henry's office was down in the same quarters, or in the vicinity, anyhow. I got on the wrong-way traffic; there was one-way traffic there. I stopped and said, "Oh, oh, we're going the wrong way." He said, "Let's go anyhow, and see what will happen." So we went down and caused a lot of commotion. People were hollering, "Hey, where you going?" until they saw Mr. Ford. We went over to this little Congregational Church on

Rotunda Drive. He didn't get out of the car, as he had on his bedroom slippers. But he did speak to the preacher.

Rankin concludes:

We came down Southfield, and there was a big freight train there. It was just making it; the wheels were just turning. He said, "Wait a minute. Let's see if this fellow is going to make it or not." The engine was going on the railroad there, coming upgrade. He said, "Well, I guess it's going to make it." So we pulled into the house. I got him home at 3:15, and he was as bright as a dollar. He said, "Good night," and he would see me in the morning at breakfast time.

Ford had returned home to find the floodwaters greatly receded and the men in the powerhouse on the verge of restoring electrical power. When they did, Ford joked with the men that he was going to tell Clara that he himself had made the repairs.[14-1] After a routine evening of listening to his favorite radio shows, the power went down again and Ford went to bed with only the rudiments of civilization—a candle and a fireplace. His death that night by cerebral brain hemorrhage came swiftly. As Ford lingered momentarily, cradled in his wife's arms, Rosa Buhler, their German-born maid of more than a decade, responded to the summons of Clara Ford, pausing to pray for a moment outside the door. Part of Rosa's oral history tells the remainder of the story. Rosa says to Clara Ford:

"Well, the doctor will be here soon. Maybe it would be good if you went to get dressed. And later on, when you come back, I'll go and dress." So she [Clara Ford] went to her dressing room to put a dress on. He [Henry Ford] was very quiet. But, I could see the change, you know, on his face. I noticed the peace coming over Mr. Ford. He was at peace, yes. Because while Mrs. Ford dressed, I stood at the end of his bed, and I was concerned somehow or another, to know if he was at peace with God. And I prayed to myself and said, "Dear God, give me the assurance that all is well between you and Mr. Ford." And

then I had such a feeling of peace come over me. And he [Henry Ford] raised his hands up and folded them. And then I felt as if he were saying to me, "Don't ever leave Mrs. Ford." You know, he didn't say it aloud, but as if he in his spirit were telling me that. And I heard myself say aloud, "No, I won't leave her." I have never told anyone that before.

Rosa continues:

And I said to Mrs. Ford, "You had better come." And she said, "What do you think it is?" I said, "I think Mr. Ford is leaving us." And she couldn't grasp it. I then sent the watchman over to get Thompson. Mrs. Ford sat on the bed, but she couldn't grasp the fact that Mr. Ford was gone. Thompson asked if he could see Mr. Ford. After that, he went to the front door to be there when Dr. Mateer arrived. Mrs. Ford said to Dr. Mateer, "Buhler tells me that Mr. Ford has left us." And the doctor examined Mr. Ford. The doctor said, "I think I'll call the *Detroit News*." And I said to Mrs. Ford, "Don't you think you should let young Mr. Henry [Henry II] know first?" And she said, "Oh, of course, I wasn't thinking. Yes."

The significance of the *Detroit News* being notified first expresses the idea that Henry Ford belonged to the world. A visitor to Fair Lane with a strong ethnic background once commented that in ancient times, the death of a great man was often marked by a dramatic, natural disaster. The lightning bolt that destroyed the large tree outside Carl Jung's deathbed comes to mind. Jung opened up/split open the human mind as the lightning bolt split open the ancient tree. For Henry Ford, it was the flood of the century, a flood that spread and covered much of his empire, swamping his *Suwanee* riverboat in Greenfield Village and rendering all of his backup systems useless. Our rational, empirical minds quickly discount these happenings as random coincidental acts of nature, but perhaps we miss a symbolism that could easily be deduced from these events. Newspaper headlines come closest to such interpretations: "The mechanical genius born by candlelight, dies by candlelight."

Looking more specifically at the cause agent, the flood, we could applaud the Almighty's choice of commemorative acts. The flood of mass manufactured items that Ford's perfection of the moving assembly line has given this century and those yet to come certainly is epochal. Thanks to Henry Ford and the brains and brawn he harnessed, we are indeed living after that "flood," that deluge.

Perhaps Ford's death was, after all, in God's good time. One day, Ford had asked a visiting Episcopal priest, "Do you think God intended me all along to build the car?" Perhaps not, but perhaps it was a way to build a car that changed the world forever. As Will Rogers said of Ford, "One hundred years from now, we'll know whether he helped us or hurt us, but he didn't leave us where he found us."

Eternal Flames

After Henry died, Clara Ford became more and more bound by the walls of the spacious master bedroom suite where, on April 7, 1947, being kept warm by the fireplace, the dying embers illuminated her beloved lifelong mate's last moments.

Clara lived for three more years after Henry's death, passing away in 1950. The suite where she last held Henry became her home. The rest of the house became abandoned. Her own study became a storeroom. Even her gardens lost their charm and her attentions. For the most part, Clara would venture outdoors only through the use of binoculars, calling down to her faithful servants to report a gardener not performing his duty. Workers who had the responsibility of mowing the long meadow that stretched out in view of her bedroom windows devised a clever means of switching drivers so they could take their break out of view of Mrs. Ford.

The Ford grandchildren all were grown and married. Clara's first great-grandchild, Charlotte Ford, had continued the Santa's Workshop

This is Clara and Henry Ford's master bedroom, in its last incarnation with twin beds. In later years, Clara is said to have opted for a good night's sleep instead of sleeping with her husband. In Henry's last years, a series of strokes made him increasingly restless at night. (Photograph from the Collections of Henry Ford Museum & Greenfield Village)

tradition at Christmas and visited the Estate, probably bringing great joy to her elderly great-grandmother. Clara's niece, Fran ImOberstag, and her children brought a parrot as a gift to Clara from their home across the river, to help break the loneliness. Clara continued to spend summers at the Huron Mountain Club and winters at Richmond Hill, but her heart was no longer in anything, except perhaps her church, Christ Episcopal on North Military Avenue in Dearborn. Clara had helped turn the spade and had donated to its construction. Henry Ford had tried to influence the design of the church but was rebuffed by the rector. Although he was an experienced church builder, Ford's history of nonsectarianism and the blending of religious tradition was not acceptable. Thus, Clara had the honor of turning the spade.

As Clara spent many of the final months of her life in the master bedroom suite, her loneliness was eased by Polly the parrot, to whom she would talk. The bird would talk to Clara also and surprised many a servant. Polly indeed was a pretty bird, and Clara gave it the run of Fair Lane. Perhaps the rawness of the bird's squawk reminded Clara of the raw times Henry and she went through to surmount the mountain of a life they had lived together. The parrot's raspy voice certainly did not remind Clara of Henry's whistle, which had been so full, vibrant, and bird-like, and had filled the main entrance hall each day. Therefore, while Clara wrote letters to dear friends of happy days, whose memories still filled the place, Polly squawked away some of the gloom that overhung the room in which Henry had died. In one letter from these sunset times, Clara wrote,

Santa's Workshop is held this year again, but we miss him...

We do not know if Clara's thoughts were for the future of her beloved Fair Lane. Henry had been more direct, at one time saying,

It will all go to hell after I'm gone. [14-2]

Perhaps Clara thought that young Henry [Henry Ford II] would tend to things and that the Ford Foundation, with all its millions, would do what was needed for the Village and Fair Lane. The place had been Clara's home for more than 30 years. Some, including Henry, had said it was too big, but Clara had loved it, gardens and all.

In Clara's will, the lawyers had even misspelled Fair Lane; they made it one word. It was the first of many insults that would require the attention of new generations of Fords to correct.

Fair Lane had been a good home. The Fords had shared many joys there, and they had shared them with a great many people. Clara once said that she knew from the moment she met Henry Ford that God had something special in mind for him. Clara was lonely but at peace, a

peace she probably felt even more at Christmas. Clara remembered to ensure that Christ Episcopal Church received the crèche set she and Henry had bought in Oberamergau in 1930. Every ten years, this village has put on the Passion Play of Christ in thanks for the deliverance of their ancestors from the plague in medieval times. What a wondrous trip that had been! Clara had never seen Henry so taken by the Christian religion and the man who portrayed Christ in the play. Clara was as much a collector as Henry had been. Her study became filled with these bygone treasures, to the point that nieces referred to her study as "Clara's junk room."

Henry Ford had hoped to live to be 100 years old; however, at the age of 83, he was dead of a cerebral hemorrhage far short of his goal. His wife Clara died three years later at 83 also. Both are remembered as saints and sinners. Clara was never an easy taskmaster—whether it was to a white foreman at Richmond Hill, Georgia, who received her firm and forceful advice on how to treat his African-American workers with respect, or the gardeners at Fair Lane, who much preferred Henry to visit. Clara called them and even Henry to account, perhaps because her religious training told her that she too would be held accountable for all the power and riches they enjoyed. The tunnel pipes in the passageway between her greenhouse and the residence at Fair Lane were kept white-glove clean—not simply to praise God with cleanliness but to exhibit Clara's stewardship of her wealth.

Henry Ford had taken a more *laissez-faire* approach to money, routinely leaving his daily cash allowance stuck in his clothes or between library books. In effect, Henry continued to live as if he had no more money than anyone else. In later years, Ford delighted in exhibiting how much money he did not have. Perhaps his self-delusion was a result of not becoming wealthy until middle age.

Set among Ford's other actions are traces of both irreverence and irresponsibility. Unlike Clara, Henry Ford for a time acted toward his closest associates as if he was not accountable to anyone. One phrase comes to mind: "Power corrupts. Absolute power corrupts absolutely." Henry Ford's power was as absolute in his kingdom as any monarch until the United Auto Workers (UAW) challenged and won the right to represent Ford workers in 1941, around the time of Ford's first strokes and the beginning of his demise. Prior to settling, Ford had not only resisted but proclaimed he would not settle "until hell froze over."

Howard Simpson, Ford's tractor engineer, praised Ford for his leadership and treatment of his workers in the 1914–1915 period of the labor strike. However, Simpson felt that Ford began acting as if he were a "demigod" in the 1920s and 1930s, when Simpson worked at Fair Lane and in the Ford research laboratories.

Furthermore, Simpson felt Ford's actions in this manner were exacerbated rather than grounded when Ford was personally exposed to the preaching of Frank Buchman of the Moral Rearmament Association. Both the Fords and the Simpsons became followers of this Presbyterian minister, who preached peace through reaffirmation of a nonsectarian religious moral revival. Specifically, Simpson felt that Ford misinterpreted Buchman's Biblical reference to the guiding hand of God. Divine guidance became divine license, and Simpson recoiled at the manipulative way Ford sometimes treated his engineers.

Jim Newton knew Henry Ford for two decades and maintains that Ford questioned but always remained firm in his Christian beliefs.

Whether Ford read his Bible every day as he professed late in life in many sources is not as important as what Ford lived. People experienced Ford in his last decades of life in varying fashions. When I responded to an inquiry from an Estate tour guest as to what Ford's religious beliefs were, the guest replied, "Ford was baptized and buried a Christian…and was a lot things in between." At the end of that tour, another guest firmly set me straight. Early in her life, this woman had attended the Ford school at Greenfield Village, and she felt I had given Mr. Ford "short shrift" when it came to Ford's religious beliefs. She protested that she saw Henry Ford attend chapel every day with the students. At Berry College, a cameraman captured on film both Clara and Henry Ford flanking Martha Berry during a chapel service. Clara was not singing, but Martha Berry and Henry Ford were. As family members recall, Clara was much more devotional. However, Jim Newton, now well into his nineties, never doubted the depth of Henry Ford's Christian soul.

Ford did not live to be 100 years old as he had hoped, but he did live long enough to ask for and celebrate the "amazing grace" that can in part explain and forgive his triumphs and failures. Perhaps at places such as Berry College, the Greenfield Village Chapel, and Richmond Hill, Henry Ford gave his praise and allegiance to serve God. Then, at other times and similar to so many of us great and small, Ford sang only to the camera of public opinion and/or our baser instincts.

THE BALLAD OF HENRY FORD

Music & lyrics by Donn P. Werling

Let me tell you the stor - y of Hen - ry Ford: A-
round him you were nev-er bored. He am - mend - ed mil- lions & of-
fend-ed some, But you can't do ny what he has done.

His first memory was that of a bird
Walking through the fields, the song that he heard
Of a white crowned sparrow defending its young
He said he always remembered its song.

He never had much of an education
But he made millions from his vocation
Hands on, by the bootstraps, but never bootless
Except when a vision hit him square in the guts

For guts he had for good or for bad
Saving the birds when most thought him mad
His five dollar day offended the rich
But stopping WWI got him into a fix

He heard it was rich Jews who were to blame
He hated money men so old prejudice became
A pitfall to him, all financiers were Jews
Until a Jewish friend got him out of his stew

His neighbor Rabbi Franklin couldn't take anymore
He sent back the seventh free car to Ford's store
Ford called him to ask why he was in such a lather
The Rabbi replied with his wise gray matter

Dr. Franklin looked those free cars in the eye
And Ford responded as I hope you and I
An apology came, the Independent was defamed
And Ford threw his money down other lanes.

Dr. Carver of Tuskegee fame
And Martha Berry, educators the same
Helping rural people, but mostly the young
With an education...how the new south begun.

Clara Ford was his wife's name.
He called her Callie. She guided his fame.
She was the believer and mother of his child.
She steered a steady course-kept Henry from the wild.

From the T back to the A the car business he reordered
His powerful V-8 set his cornerstone in mortar
The Fordson tractor and plastic cars too
He put soybeans into cars if they were too hard to chew.

His railroads and planes; he had the Midas touch
And when the stock market fell he left most in his dust
He turned to preserving the common man's past
When most thought it foolish to be concerned with trash.

Old inns and water mills were his favorites to restore
Followed by schools and one thing more
He built seven chapels and attended every day
In his last decades of steeled hair gray

Music and dance were his avocation
Revival of the tunes and steps to all locations
Long before Nashville he searched all around
For the fiddlers and bands that played the old sound.

Ford, Ford millions more of everything
Except fall, summer, winter or spring
Time will be the final judge
How much was steel, how much was gold
How much of his life like us he fudged?

So Mr. Ford, we will leave you to the ages
Even though you might not be counted with the sages,
A thousand years from now when all is said and done
Kettering has said you will be our brightest son

Ford, Ford, mass manufacturing
Cheaper, lighter with quality's ring! Make it
stronger to last longer. Be stewards of the past.
Help the other fella with true charity that lasts.

CHAPTER FIFTEEN

EBB POWER: THE FORD LEGACY IN THE BALANCE

1861–1865	*Civil War*
1863	Henry Ford's birth
1888	Marriage to Clara Bryant
1893	Birth of Edsel Ford
1896	Quadricycle
	(First vehicle built by Henry Ford)
	First met Thomas Edison
	First met Harvey Firestone
1899	Detroit Automobile Company founded
1902	Henry Ford Company formed
1903	Ford Motor Company founded
1908	Model T
1912	First met John Burroughs
1913	Moving assembly line
	Migratory Bird Act passed
1914	$5 a day wage
	First met Jack Miner
1914–1918	*World War I*
1915	Fair Lane completed
	Bought the bungalow in the Upper Peninsula
1916	Bought home in Ft. Myers
1917	Fordson tractor
	Birth of Henry Ford II, the first of four grandchildren
1918	Migratory Bird Treaty with Canada
1918–1924	"Four Vagabonds" camping trips
1919	Ford sole owner of Ford Motor Company
1919–1927	X engine (The engine/car that never was)
1921	First met Martha Berry
1922	Lincoln Motor Company purchased
1924	Built first diesel freighters on the Great Lakes
1925	Admitted to Huron Mt. Club
	Began acquiring Georgia land
1926	Ford Tri-motor
1927	Model A introduced; Model T discontinued
1929	Greenfield Village/Museum dedicated
1929–1941	*The Great Depression*
1932	Ford V-8
1935	Built Richmond Hill
1937	Battle of the Overpass—U.A.W.
1939–1945	*World War II*
1940	Henry Ford II and Anne McDonnell marry
1941	First plastic car (soybeans)
	Ford signs with the U.A.W.
	Birth of Charlotte Ford, first great-grandchild
1943	Death of Edsel Ford
1947	Death of Henry Ford
1948	Edsel Ford II born to Mr. and Mrs. Henry Ford II
1950	Death of Clara Ford

Forty miles south of Ford's Richmond Hill in Georgia, pioneer sawyers as early as 1716 tapped the power of the tides—the power of the ebb. When the six-foot to nine-foot tides were at their highest, the water was trapped in specially constructed tidal ponds and then slowly released to turn the undershot (hydropower feed from below, instead of on top, which is overshot) water wheels. The drudgery of pit sawing the logs into planks was thus eliminated through mechanization using the fullness of the sea.

In the usual sense of the word "ebb," we often speak of life as wasting away. In these early tidal mills, ebb meant power. How much ebb and power did this tide leave? We can ask the same of our respective lives on this earth. Henry Ford's life had ebb power, and that is perhaps most often and dramatically demonstrated in the continued power and influence that his company holds, as the most successful and largest family-controlled company in all recorded history. Few farmers' sons have reached so far and so deeply into the lives of people around the world.

Mediocre lives have much less ebb power and leave few legacies. Ford left many legacies. Some are from the high tide of his life, and others are from his low watermarks. In some situations, an action viewed as a strength might, in other times and circumstances, be a decided weakness. Thus, this summary overview and review of Ford's life, his high points and low points, reflects the hearthside perspective of the book. In total, Ford is viewed as having left a dozen major legacies as high points and four low watermarks. In his much beloved *McGuffey Readers* books, each book offers lessons to be learned. So too does Ford's life offer lessons to be learned: some with power, and some simply a reminder that Henry Ford, similar to each of us, had feet of clay.

Ford, a hero of labor in the early 1900s, became a villain of labor—especially organized labor—in the 1930s and afterward. An innovator on one of the largest scales in world history, he acquired a Model T image that perhaps may have been undeserved. Nonetheless, that image of Ford is firmly implanted in contemporary society. Ford's efforts to revitalize old-time dancing, during this same time when the

successor to the Model T was delayed time and again, synergized negatively to drop Ford from the cutting edge to the trailing edge. His work with the soybean and plastics was a notable exception.

Change began to pass Ford by during a period of accelerated change, the pace of which he and his company had helped to create. In some things, such as his ban on smoking, Ford appeared to his contemporaries as being personally vindictive against those who were not like him.[15-1] The growth and success of Ford's own company was perhaps his greatest challenge and downfall. With the genius of organizational management such as Alfred P. Sloan at its helm, General Motors surpassed Ford. Sloan also was ahead of his time. Regarding other examples, such as labor relations, we could say the same. Ford's firm simply grew too large to maintain the heady heyday of the Piquette Avenue plant, Highland Park, and especially the Rouge plant. In some ways, Ford's tremendous commitment to chemurgy, decentralization, and his Village Industries program (green field factories) was his answer to not only keeping "one foot in the soil," but to returning to a simpler time because it was more human in scale. In Ford's view and in the view of countless modern-day managers of decentralized factories, they and their employees work better because of their suburban or exurban work environments.

Bitterness about Ford's stand on no public charity in the face of the Ford hunger march of the 1930s, when Communist organizers and laid-off Ford workers marched in protest, is confusing to me. I have seen and heard documentary evidence of Ford's many private but large-scale and often confidential acts of behind-the-scenes philanthropy. Ford's respect for the common man on both a human and spiritual level would not allow him, whatever the public relations costs, to greet the Ford hunger marchers by opening his checkbook and popping his suspenders in front of the camera. To do so publicly would have made Ford into something he loathed. From his perspective, the public recipients of such charity would become recipients of a "fish" that would be gone tomorrow, as opposed to spending time and resources on finding new renewable resource markets for a new and more productive way of fishing or farming.

Many people believe the Rouge plant was one of both Ford's and America's greatest achievements—an industrial site so renowned that a million visitors tour it annually. Even today, many call it America's equivalent to the pyramids of Egypt. If the pyramids were the emblem chosen for our dollar bills, the Rouge plant was the prototype for the factories that generated the wealth that made the United States many times richer than all the gold in all the tombs in the pyramids of that ancient land.

In one important way, the Rouge plant is similar to Ford's marital infidelity with Evangeline Dahlinger and makes him a hypocrite. The Rouge plant was first financed with the war effort defense money of World War I. What is worse is that it was not his, but the government's. It is true that the Eagle boat (a submarine chaser built on an assembly line) was produced here, and it is true that Ford risked his newly gained financial security by transforming the Rouge plant into more than a war production facility.

In many ways, Ford himself was the financial manipulator he came to despise. The social cost of gathering eighty-five thousand people in one spot weighed heavily on Ford. He developed his Village Industries Program of decentralization as an alternative, or at least complementary, model. Which course was best for humankind in the long run remains to be decided. Presently, the world is voting for decentralization. Urban design critics and visionary architects such as Paolo Soleri would argue that a cleaned-up, concentrated industrial base such as Ford created at the Rouge plant is the prototype. The "3 R's" of Ford and his contemporaries, not McGuffey, were and remain: reduce, reuse, and recycle. These are more feasible in centralization than in scattered village industry plants that generate exurban sprawl. In building the Rouge plant, Ford, an avid birder, smothered a great birding site. He also built a model that industrial leaders from around the world came to see. The Rouge plant became synonymous with American might.

Henry Ford walked through the tunnel connecting his powerhouse to his residence at Fair Lane to measure the deepest spot underground where he could seek shelter from Hitler's rockets. They might never

Here at the mighty Rouge plant, almost a hundred thousand workers turned raw materials into cars and, in the war years, jeeps and tanks. It was a linchpin in making Detroit the "Arsenal of Democracy" for victory during two world wars because tanks, jeeps, and boats all were built there. Today, the Rouge plant—along with Greenfield Village and Fair Lane, the Henry Ford Estate—are National Historic Landmarks. They are part of the Rouge River corridor, which Congress designated in 1998 as part of the National Automobile Heritage Area. (Photograph from the Collections of the Henry Ford Estate. George Ebling, Jr., photographer)

target Ford's home, but a key element of the arsenal of democracy was Ford's Rouge plant four miles downstream. Unlike many modern industrialists, Henry Ford lived practically next door to his plant. When the wind blows from the southeast at Fair Lane, the Henry Ford estate, you can still smell Ford's mightiest creation. Similar to Montgomery Ward, who helped create Chicago's sparkling lakefront from the worn-out refuse of the Chicago fire, Ford bloomed where he was planted. He may have had north woods and subtropical retreats, but he lived in Dearborn. Building his grand estate in Dearborn did not attract other millionaires because Ford's land abutted middle-class and even low-class housing developments.

Two historic markers presently interpret the Rouge complex. One will someday be added if the National Park Service study on labor-related historic sites is completed. The new marker will tell the story of the 1937 Battle of the Overpass when Harry Bennett's force brutalized Walter Reuther and other U.A.W. representatives, other labor tensions, and the resultant tragedies of an aging manipulative owner, Henry Ford, who gave titles but not real authority to his son Edsel and could not let go. Instead, Henry Ford worked to undermine what authority he delegated by counteractions executed through his company strongman and head of security, Harry Bennett. Some of the complexities of the relationship between Ford and Bennett were discussed in a previous chapter of this book. Even more than his anti-Semitism, Ford's interactions with his son Edsel are one of the great enigmas of Ford's life. Henry Ford deeply loved his son. Bob Smith said that the day Edsel died, the sparkle left Ford's eyes. For those who loved the Fords, Henry's actions toward Edsel were a bitter cup that was and remains hard to swallow.

Some scholars have argued recently that the Irish-Americans made it into mainstream America at the expense of African-Americans. Henry Ford, an Irish-American, has been called "...a great benefactor of the Negro race, probably the greatest that ever lived."[15-2] Ford had an abiding prejudice that Jewish financiers achieved success at the expense of Gentile labor and innovation. Ford apologized to his neighbor, the esteemed Rabbi Leo Franklin, who refused his seventh free car from Ford and returned it. Ford apologized nationally for the anti-

Semitic articles published in the *Dearborn Independent*. Did Ford ever break free of his prejudice? It is doubtful. To say that Ford's prejudice was limited to financiers, whom he called Jewish due to his uneducated nineteenth-century background, is not being fair to either Gentiles or Jews who, by the millions, refused to sip from the pot of prejudice.

The greatest story is too often missed in the aftertaste of Ford's anti-Semitism. Perhaps it did not exact a full cure, but it was a friend and neighbor who put aside personal favors—not small ones then or now—and called Ford to account. Jewish biographers and authors have never been kind to Ford for reasons that are understandable. Rabbi Leo Franklin was a leader of Reformed Judaism, and perhaps because of his reformed status, the significance of the rabbi's actions has been slighted. How we stop prejudice is a question to which the rabbi's actions give both answers and an example worth repeating to new generations. Rabbi Franklin did more than refuse to accept Ford's seventh free car; he held Ford's actions up to Ford's nose and, in so many words, said, "I know you are better than your recent actions have portrayed you." The rabbi passed the ultimate test of friendship. He confronted Ford when Ford was wrong because he had lived with Ford as a neighbor and had accepted not only six free cars but experienced sincerity and genuineness as well. Margaret Fleischaker, Rabbi Franklin's daughter, recalled [15-3] sitting in their Ford on Woodward in front of the old temple. Her father was not having much success in cranking the engine until Henry Ford pulled over, got out, and started the engine for them. Ford's apology to the Jewish people was largely or entirely written by others. However, his many gifts to the world, including his vision of a car for the masses, were hands-on, similar to the simple act of taking his own hand and starting the car for a neighbor and friend.

Not One, But Five Halls of Fame

Automotive and Auto Sports Halls of Fame

We would expect Henry Ford to be in the Automotive Hall of Fame. For those who know how he first gained fame, his induction into the

Auto Sports Hall of Fame is not surprising. Ford loved to race. Although he once set the world land speed record, he soon abandoned his personal physical involvement in racing. Nonetheless, Ford never gave up his love of racing on foot.

National Inventors Hall of Fame

Critics who say Ford never invented anything but merely fed off the minds of others may be surprised to learn that Ford is in the National Inventors Hall of Fame. The induction credentials cite Ford's transmission mechanism, Patent No. 1005186 in particular, but the following citation is perhaps more important:

> Pioneering automotive engineer Henry Ford held many patents on automotive mechanisms but is best remembered for helping devise the factory assembly approach to production that revolutionized the auto industry by greatly reducing the time required to assemble a car."[15-4]

Aviation Hall of Fame

The Aviation Hall of Fame recognition of Henry Ford is not surprising because many people today remember taking their first airplane ride on the legendary Ford Tri-motor. What is surprising is the long list of other successes that the Aviation Hall of Fame included in its description of Ford's aviation achievements. Below is a small fraction of Ford's achievements [15-5] that put him beside the Wright Brothers and Charles Lindbergh:

> ...like the early successful automobiles, the early successful airplanes found little public acceptance. They were unsafe, underpowered, and not capable of serving the needs of the general population of the world. It was Henry Ford who pioneered the successful adaptation of the basic concept of the airplane and thus brought aviation and its advantages within the reach of the average citizen. It was his efforts in developing suitable aircraft to serve the public, and then building public confidence in their reliability, safety, and public necessity, that put the nation on wings.

> His [Ford's] contributions were far more than simple financial support. He took a look at the whole sphere of influence which the infant aviation industry was creating in a haphazard fashion, and then drew up his own blueprint for its future...a future that required not only safe, dependable aircraft, but also facilities to properly help them serve the public.

> But when the Great Depression settled on the world, the Ford Tri-motor, noisy but ever faithful, went out of production and became a legend in aviation history. Even today, however, a nostalgic affection persists about the grand old "Tin Goose." Tales galore are told about her many and varied accomplishments.

> For Henry Ford, the passing of the Ford Tri-motor was not the end of his involvement in aviation. He had built a Ford "Flivver" midget plane that promised to bring the personal aircraft within the grasp of the average person. His concept was sound, but his timing was bad. Twenty years later, airports all over the world would be lined with such small aircraft, owned and operated by a new generation that had discovered the age-old thrill of personal flight.

> Then, when World War II burst upon the nation, Henry Ford, the pacifist at heart, rolled up his sleeves and turned his energies toward the building of thousands of Pratt & Whitney "Double Wasp" aircraft engines and B-24 "Liberator" bombers that helped wring victory over a tyranny that had sought to engulf the world.

The *New York Times* credits Ford with the development of the systems of modern commercial aviation. From concrete runways to reliability tests to an airport hotel, Ford was first or often ahead of his time.

The Mamajuda Lighthouse once lit the path for Great Lakes vessels on the Detroit River. In Henry Ford's youth, the lighthouse was tended by Barney and Caroline Litogot, Ford's uncle and aunt. The lighthouse keeper and civil war veteran probably regaled young Henry Ford with tales of the Civil War. He also must have pointed out the boom in Great Lakes commerce that sailed by the lighthouse doorstep fewer than ten miles from Ford's Dearborn farm. The boom was only beginning. (Photograph from the Collection of the Great Lakes Lighthouse Keepers Association)

Along with the **Benson Ford,** *the* **Henry Ford II** *(shown here) was the first of Ford's great lake boats, equipped with diesels and state-of-the-art advances for navigation on the Great Lakes. In 1988, Henry Ford was admitted into the National Maritime Hall of Fame. (Photograph from the George Ebling Collection of the Henry Ford Institute)*

National Maritime Hall of Fame

Ford's induction into the National Maritime Hall of Fame is perhaps even more of a surprise, as much for the reasons given for his inclusion. In 1988, six years after this hall of fame formed, Henry Ford was inducted not because he owned one of the largest fleets of privately owned boats ever assembled, but because of his innovations. His Eagle boat/submarine chaser was mass produced for World War I. The *Henry Ford II*, and the *Benson Ford* were among the first vessels to use diesel propulsion on the Great Lakes. Likewise, the strategic location of Ford's factories took advantage of land and sea connections. These were among the reasons cited for why this nephew of a lighthouse keeper became a mogul and master of the land, sea, and air.

National Agricultural Hall of Fame

The National Agricultural Hall of Fame has not yet inducted Henry Ford. However, a list of Ford's agricultural achievements with the Fordson tractor, the soybean, and his popularization of the three-point hitch suggested to the current director that Ford's nomination would be seriously considered. Perhaps even more revolutionary than the Fordson tractor in terms of design was Ford Model 9N, first produced in 1939 with a Ferguson three-point hitch and hydraulic system. Ford directed his engineers to ignore the competition. In so doing, Ford set the pattern for tractor design into the present day. Both Ford and

Ferguson also had agreed that the tractor should be operable by women and children. It was.[15-6] Similar to the Automotive Hall of Fame, which recently inducted individuals from the earliest days of the automotive industry because no one had nominated them previously, a nomination of Henry Ford to the National Agricultural Hall of Fame is now past due.

Similar to the publication of *Who's Who* books, halls of fame can become infamous for their fecundity. However, the ones discussed here are "the real McCoys." Each has either been chartered by its industry or Congress. Inclusion in any one is a seminal honor. Inclusion in five with the sixth pending is unheard of and gives credence to the *Life* magazine ranking of Henry Ford with the Edisons, DaVincis, and Isaac Newtons of this past millennium.

Preservation Hall of Fame

The Edison Institute (Museum and Greenfield Village) was to be Henry Ford's grand tribute to history that was not bunk. Ford often was quoted as saying that the evolution of the plow had a much greater impact on civilization than the evolution and glorification of wars and battles that had been the stuff of history lessons and tests for centuries. In the beginning, it was to be a tribute to the hands-on inventive genius of Thomas Alva Edison. Although the Edison Institute name survives, few know of its continued existence. Renamed in Ford's honor as the Henry Ford Museum and Greenfield Village, the name of Edison has been backstaged; however, the spirit of change and discovery for children of all ages endures.

Over the years, the village has been criticized both internally and externally by the media and Fordophiles for not respecting the museum as a sacrosanct creation of Henry Ford. In recent years, much moving and many transfers of structures in and out have occurred to improve both

The largest indoor-outdoor museum in the world was built by Henry Ford across the railroad tracks from his Estate. It tells the history of how far and how fast we have come, with an emphasis on the spirit of innovation. The museum was dedicated to the memory of Thomas Edison. However, today it is called the Henry Ford Museum and Greenfield Village, in honor of its creator who welcomed the world—including a young Walt Disney— to enjoy history the way Ford thought it should be taught. (Photograph from the Collections of Henry Ford Museum & Greenfield Village)

The Correct Name is "THE EDISON INSTITUTE" the 'Museum' & the 'Village' are subparts—

the content and delivery of its story. The auto exhibit in the museum has become more professional; no longer are there the rows upon rows of antique cars that made it a collector's delight and a lay visitor's bane. The improvements are legion and generally have been applauded; however, some people question all the progress and express the desire that it should become a museum of a museum dedicated to Ford's genius as expressed in the museum field.

Once tractors, camping trucks, the quadricycle, the 999 race car, and a succession of automobiles (first a Model T, then a Model A, and finally a V-8) filled this space. The garage also housed bicycles for Ford and others, particularly children, to take up Ford's exercise regime of riding four miles daily. Today, thousands of tourists come to the garage to hear its story. (Photograph from the Collections of the Henry Ford Estate)

this proves that Henry Ford's rows upon rows of antique cars or famous people's houses are not relevant to everyday life unless their history is interpreted and revealed.

Unlike the Banff Natural History Museum in which time has been frozen since approximately 1900, it is doubtful Henry Ford intended to freeze history from the onset. At Greenfield Village and in the Henry Ford Museum, Ford tinkered with history and its interpretation as he did with cars. There was plenty of room for disagreement, on both the details and the substance. Workers came to know that Henry and Clara Ford had differing tastes and kept flats of flowers ready to change the floral composition of the Cotswold Cottage gardens, depending on whether it was Henry or Clara who was expected. In many ways, the Henry Ford Museum (as it is now called) and Greenfield Village was and continues to be a pioneering venture to pull together the threads of what causes change. In the Menlo Park laboratory where Edison perfected the light bulb, Ford was more conservative. After Edison stood up from reenacting his invention of the light bulb, Ford had the chair on which Edison had sat nailed to the floor, presumably to never move again. Edison's final seat, similar to his final breath, was substantive to Henry Ford.

In Banff, Canada, a "museum" of a museum (circa 1904) exists and takes visitors back to the turn of the century. There are no cars—only mounts of deer, elk, bear, and the like. For all its preserved quaintness, the Banff museum remains attractive to visitors today perhaps because many of the specimens are full-body mounts and represent a population of animals that can be found today in the surrounding Canadian wilderness. Ford's pioneering work in the museum field enabled him to assemble a collection of cars as complete as the collection of animals that turn-of-the-century hunters compiled for the Banff natural history museum. However, even in Dearborn, with its old-car festivals and its antique-car lovers, we are seldom surprised outside Greenfield Village by the beep of an old, rare Ford car. The bugle of the elk remains a common and expected occurrence in Banff. All of

We can debate the historical accuracy of omitting homes and businesses of accountants and, other than Abraham Lincoln, lawyers from Greenfield Village. However, the success of Ford's pioneering venture cannot be denied. Rockefeller may have spent as much or more money saving an important colonial town called Williamsburg, but in recent years, Henry Ford's outdoor and indoor museum of Americana has drawn thousands more visitors. Colonial Williamsburg was and is a real town; Ford's Greenfield Village is fictional with a historic assemblage of structures and artifacts. Colonial Williamsburg helps document the founding of this country; Ford intended to demonstrate the founding of modern life from its humble origins.

Henry Ford probably will be associated with his quote that "History is bunk!" until the end of time. However, if Ford's descendants have anything to say about it, and they very much do, the tinkering with historical preservation and interpretation will continue as well. Henry Ford has seldom been given credit for the bold strokes he made in the field of historic preservation and interpretation, whether it was cars or kitchens where he did a better job of interpreting history. That recognition too often has been controlled by the East Coast society, which dabbled and dipped into its pockets to advance historic preservation in towns a century or more older than Dearborn, Michigan. Ford not only dipped; he dove into his deep pockets, to a total sum that will probably never be fully accounted. The fortune he spent was staggering. Ford did not dabble like a duck; he tinkered like the mechanic he was. Mechanistic, hands-on, utilitarian history was what Ford sought.

Social historians who ascribe progress to the convergence of being at the right time and in the right place with the right idea with which the times are pregnant had not fully emerged in Ford's time. Ford would have agreed with Harold Shapiro, former president of the University of Michigan and now president at Princeton University, that the actions of individuals rather than random convergence of possibilities bring about technological and civilizational advance. In Shapiro's Ford Foundation-funded sabbatical study of what caused the pulse of change, he concluded that seven other places in the world could possibly have become the motor capital of the world. It happened in Detroit because people such as Henry Ford made the difference.

Social historians have tended to discount the importance of individuals, especially the "great white men" of our country. Although Ford had his struggles with hubris, he remained in outlook and in action a common man who did uncommon things in so many fields of endeavor that he has been labeled by *Life, Fortune*, and others in the media as one of the most important people not only of his century but of the millennium. One thing on which critics and fans can agree is that whether it was the color of the Model T or plastic or food from the soybean, Ford was an individual who, by persistence and most often with integrity, ignored the status quo and pushed the envelope of our minds' view of history and future possibilities for all.

Hospitals

A search of the Internet did not yield any "halls of fame" for those who over the years have contributed to the building of and innovations in the building of churches or hospitals. Perhaps because their calling is deemed so full of mercy, to name one individual or group of individuals above others would be sacrilegious. Henry and Clara Ford would be candidates if there were such halls of fame—not simply because they gave significant financial support to the building of facilities of mercy, but because they threw their respective genius and ingenuity into making benchmark contributions, some of which are coming into widespread appreciation only today.

The building of Detroit's first large general hospital had been stymied for years because of lack of funds. When Henry Ford volunteered to make it happen, he did so with firm convictions in mind. Some of those convictions stemmed from the pricing policies and the lack of privacy that his wife Clara had endured in a hospital stay for a hysterectomy in 1908. Having only recently made any real money, Ford was shocked at the cost of Clara's hospital stay. Pricing policies for hospitals relied on soaking the rich to pay for the poor. Ford felt that one person's appendix removal should not be different in price or service from another's. Thus, Ford was among the first to apply the principles of twentieth-century business to the running of hospitals.

To sweep aside any opposition to what he had in mind, Ford donated the entire amount necessary to create a state-of-the-art facility. Twenty-four million dollars was not a small sum then or today, and the results were impressive—not only from the perspective of the physical facilities, but from the staff Ford hired and engaged. Together, these placed for years the Henry Ford Hospital directly behind the Mayo Clinic and few others in its innovative nature and advance of good medical treatment. To make that happen, Ford pulled out all the stops and left a track record that would be hard to match in terms of business involvement in advancing the medical arts.

In planning the hospital, Ford directed that the design of the building be centered around the patient rather than a fancy facade. When Ford

Ford automotive engineers helped lay the groundwork for medical engineering. Henry Ford assigned his engineers the task of developing a bed that responded to patients' needs. The development of this bed pioneered this basic medical care advance. (The patent number listed in Henry Ford's name for a "Tilting Device for Hospital Beds" is U.S. Patent #1,517,418, filed for on July 23, 1921 and issued on December 2, 1924. Photograph from the Archives of the Henry Ford Health System, Detroit, Michigan)

first took over the hospital project, a cartoonist poked fun at Ford and his new hospital by drawing patients in motorized beds engaged in "bumper beds." Ford's beds were hand-cranked, but they were revolutionary in the new degree of patient comfort they offered. No Model T engine roared to life; however, in what may have been Ford's greatest contribution to physical improvement for patients, his engineers designed a bed that could change its shape to match the patient's desires. The profile of Ford's bed that went into production by Simmons appears very similar to that found in hospitals today.

Even more closely related to hand-cranked beds was the medical progress to which Ford helped to contribute when he was a patient and had a hernia operation. Ford refused to follow the normal proce-

dure of that era and to stay in bed to allow the stitches to heal. His doctors were surprised to see Ford recover much more quickly than patients who stayed non-ambulatory. As a result, the doctors reported their findings to the medical community about their famous patient's rapid post-operative recovery and the recoveries of others who followed similar regimens. At first, the idea of getting up so soon after surgery was dismissed and even ridiculed. In the end, only the growing national reputation of the hospital helped the new post-operative treatment procedure to prevail and decades later to become the standard post-operative procedure. Henry Ford, who had a hard time standing still throughout his life, had contributed significantly to medical science and the productivity of millions of hospital patients annually. Ford probably rebelled against the doctor's orders to remain in bed because, true to the Old English phrase emblazoned on his Fair Lane main entrance hall window, he intuitively felt that lying down in a bed too long was a "bootless" waste of time. "Bootless" in the Old English meant "without profit," and Ford was determined both for himself and for his hospital to make things work in a businesslike way.

One of the greatest innovations in the hospital field that Ford used to "upset the apple cart" of the way in which traditional hospitals were run also caused other hospitals to boycott a medical gathering hosted by the Ford Hospital. At the time, the resultant embarrassment was on Henry Ford Hospital; however, in the end, Ford's ideas prevailed. The full details of this history are well told by Patricia Scollard Painter in her book, *Henry Ford Hospital, The First 75 Years.*

From the beginning, cartoonists and doctors alike were concerned that Ford would try to engineer medicine by transferring assembly-line methods to the impairment of "good" medical procedures. The "good" medical procedure toward which Ford took aim was the position that each patient's doctor—whether he or she was good or not—was a god when it came to dictating treatment. Under the leadership of Drs. Ray McClure and Frank Sladen, Henry Ford Hospital not only had a series of physicians examine every incoming patient, but, most revolutionary of all, changed the way hospital doctors were paid. No longer was their financial allegiance tied to what the individual patient could pay; rather, the general staff were salaried centrally. Thus, if in the intake examination, a doctor disclosed a problem that a specialist should examine, the hospital did not have to wait for the patient's home doctor to request the service. The efficiencies in such a system were obvious to Ford, and he insisted on improving it, regardless of the consequences.

Ford's actions created a rift in the Detroit medical community. When the Henry Ford Hospital hosted the Wayne County Medical Society to a large meeting and banquet, the hospital was slapped in the face with half-empty tables from those who resisted and resented the changes Ford was bringing. Ford took over the hospital because, similar to his vision for a car the masses could afford, he had a vision of what a hospital should be. Ford wanted a hospital where people of moderate means could receive the best possible care in a humane environment.

For Clara Ford, medical treatment did not stop at the hospital walls. Thus, the Fords' landscape architect, Jens Jensen, was hired to create beautiful views and places for residents and families to walk and stroll on the tree-shaded lawns by a lovely stone-ledged pond. Jensen also was asked to create vegetable gardens for children who came to the hospital for long-term care, so they could maintain their long-term connections to the earth and its flowers. Today, horticultural therapy is a healing profession unto itself. Jens Jensen and Clara Ford were ahead of their times as much as Henry Ford was with his adjustable bed, in his becoming ambulatory soon after surgery, or with new doctor-hospital-patient arrangements.

Many years before his 1914 takeover offer to the board of the Detroit General Hospital, Ford had promised "…to go forward with plans for a complete and creditable hospital for the benefit of Detroit." Years later, one of Ford's key medical leaders, Dr. Frank Sladen, wrote a letter of thanks to Ford, first for having the vision to see what a hospital might be, and then for engaging him in the process. Memories of the Fords regularly appearing for graduation ceremonies of nurses or simply stopping by the children's wing or the powerhouse were not so much the stuff of legend around the hospital as much as were manifestations of the Fords' caring and giving attitudes. Today, more than seventy branches of Henry Ford Hospital are listed in the Detroit phone book. One of the first branches was part of a failure, Fordlandia,

Here is a view from a patient's window at Henry Ford Hospital. Clara Ford insisted on having their new hospital landscaped by Jens Jensen, whose genius had transformed a cornfield into their great estate at Fair Lane. Jensen had long worked with Jane Addams of Hull House in Chicago in improving the physical environment of the urban poor. He felt that the environment could work with traditional medicine to hasten the restoration of both the body and the spirit. The gardens he created around the Henry Ford Hospital became a necklace of parks enjoyed by patients, residents, and their families. (Photograph from the Henry Ford Health System Archives, Detroit, Michigan)

Resembling a natural outcropping, this pond and stonework were the back-drop for countless photographs for various graduation exercises and parties. The stonework is trademark Jens Jensen and is similar to his work at Fair Lane. Expansion of the facilities eventually buried most of Jensen's work at Henry Ford Hospital under recent additions. All that remains today are mulberry trees Jensen planted for the birds, which border the north side of the hospital. Success has exacted a more painful cure, or at least one that is not tempered with the joys of gardens, ponds, and gardening. (Photograph from the Henry Ford Health System Archives, Detroit, Michigan)

The Fords and Jens Jensen felt that these vegetable gardens for patients of the Henry Ford Hospital were both productive and therapeutic. A college course in horticultural therapy had not even been imagined in 1920, but the gardens at Ford's hospital were used by both long-term patients (mostly children, many far away from their rural homes) and those that simply lay on their beds (note the girl on the bed at the far right), soaking up the sun and the sounds of fellow children growing green in a good way. (Photograph from the Henry Ford Health System Archives, Detroit, Michigan)

Ford's rubber plantation experiment in Brazil where Ford progressively attacked malaria and other tropical diseases as he did more successfully in his medical clinic at Richmond Hill in Georgia. Ford knew the value of good medicine from the pain of his youth when his mother had died in childbirth. Whether it is the picture of Ford's mother that still hangs above his bed at Fair Lane or the beautiful Linder posthumous painting of her in the Music Room, the pain of losing his mother and infant brother in childbirth endured a lifetime and was not forgotten. Ford's personal assistant, Ernest Liebold, was given the charge to make Henry Ford Hospital the best in the land. With Ford's millions and Johns Hopkins-trained physicians, Ford succeeded to an admirable degree.

Ford, the Church Builder

Henry Ford and his wife Clara built seven chapels. Most are more than large enough to be called churches. We can conjure up many reasons why the Fords built so many chapels. Clara was a devout Episcopalian. Henry enjoyed pleasing Clara and memorializing his mother. (All the chapels were named Martha Mary chapels after the first names of Clara's mother, Martha Bryant, and Henry's mother, Mary Litogot Ford.) However, the spiritual side of Henry too often is lost after wrestling with the many contradictions of his life. More than many business scions, Ford worshipped with the youth of his various communities of learning, healing, and manufacturing. Likewise, he saw the importance of worship and obeisance to God. Each chapel has a story, and a book could be written on the Ford chapels and the worship life of Ford and his communities.

Two churches built by Ford are perhaps most instructive of Ford's beliefs and actions in regard to churches and organized religion. The first instance was long remembered and passed on by the rector of Christ Episcopal Church, the Fords' home church in Dearborn. Henry and Clara Ford donated the land for the new church, but Henry Ford could not dictate the architecture of the structure. He certainly tried, but the cleric firmly rebuffed him. Perhaps Ford built so many chapels himself because of such clerical obstinacy. The second and more important instance is detailed in part as follows. The full story can be found both at the Wayside Inn archives, which are located in the basement of the Martha Mary Chapel there, or in a recent book, *Henry Ford's Boys: The Story of the Wayside Inn Boys School*. The book is insightful, not only into Ford's educational vision but also the history of the picturesque Martha Mary Chapel that surmounts both the valley and the Ford mill below it and that engaged the entire community around in its creation.

Henry and Clara Ford built seven chapels in three states. In the last decade of Henry Ford's life, attending chapel was part of his regular routine. Some critics might say it was because Ford had so much for which to atone. (Photograph from the Collections of Henry Ford Museum & Greenfield Village)

The Martha Mary Chapel at the Wayside Inn in South Sudbury, Massachusetts, was built at Ford's direction. Ford's instructions were as symbolic as the beauty of the structure that now graces a knoll slightly west of the inn of Longfellow fame. Ford seldom donated money to a project and walked away from it. Rather, he gave form and substance to it. Ford was a person who shaped the cars that shaped a civilization. In this chapel, he succeeded in shaping a community as well.

The spire of the church points upward. as is traditional in nineteenth-century Christian houses of worship. However, the directions that Ford gave to build it pointed into every household that the Wayside Inn community experiment contained. He invited them all to build the

chapel. Some ancient white pines had mounted a low hill until the hurricane of 1938 felled them as if they were a forest of matchsticks, blocking roads with the massive tree trunks. After Ford viewed the devastation, he ordered that the white pine logs be sawn into lumber that every member of the community was to use to help build the sixth Martha Mary Chapel.

This chapel follows the traditional New England lines that Ford favored in all seven of the chapels he and Clara built, and it remains nondenominational today. The daily chapel services once held there have been described by many as heavy on Methodist hymns, Episcopalian liturgy, and Bible reading, but light on sermons. Ford had a policy of no-charge hospitality at the Wayside Inn for clergy, but he disliked the divisions that he felt were caused by overly close attention to theology. Perhaps that is why long sermons seldom occurred in Ford-built houses of worship. Ford preferred to go directly to the source, and his theology was never revolutionary. However, the community building and spiritual healing that occurred, not only at the Wayside Inn but at other churches built by Ford, certainly is noteworthy. These include Camp Legion in Dearborn, Michigan, where wounded veterans received schooling and daily chapel, and Willow Run, where Ford's workers lived through a time of national crisis during World War II.

A former Ford student and later Greenfield Village employee Dall Hutchinson, thought much of Henry Ford. In a speech, Hutchinson called Ford a soft-spoken Christian gentleman who not only sought forgiveness but practiced it. When Hutchinson and his friends accidentally threw a football into the midst of a coachman's team, the elderly coachman tragically was dragged to his death by the horses, which were spooked by the football. Dall was nervous when, on the following day, Henry Ford asked him to climb into Ford's car. Ford showed Hutchinson a tractor leveling the ground, which was sodded and watered in twenty-four hours to provide a place for the boys to play without spooking the horses.

Ford's chapels were more than symbolic. Similar to the Martha Mary Chapel at the Wayside Inn, the Fords pointed to the traditional source of their faith. However, in pointing horizontally into the homes and bedrooms of all members of the community, Ford captured the essence of the Christian message: God is not only in his heaven—He is next door and can dwell in our hearts as well. Henry and Clara Ford were raised in a traditional rural community of the nineteenth century in which the church played a central role in almost every community. They spent a significant portion of their lives not only memorializing their respective mothers by building churches but by working to build community as their mothers had lived and modeled for them. Ford accomplished this the old-fashioned way at the Wayside Inn by holding a church raising. Chapel services at Richmond Hill, Georgia, were transmitted to Dearborn via radio to create a larger sense of commu-

nity via modern technology. It was anything but the New Age chapels that some businesses today provide for their employees; however, it did feed the same hunger in the soul. Although Ford had a distaste for doctrine, those who attended the many chapels for years recall Ford's active participation and satisfaction at what he had wrought in giving a place for God at the center of his communities while reaching into the hearts and souls of his neighbors and coworkers.

Conclusion

The real drama of the life of Henry Ford is not captured in the study of one man. His many achievements came from a recognition that teamwork was the key ingredient in unlocking the future. That does not imply Ford was always a good team builder. The oral histories of his engineers at Fair Lane give testimony that Ford's management of engineering teams was not always productive and sometimes backfired. In his book, *Uncommon Friends*, Jim Newton focused on his unusual life. He had been privileged to know as friends some of the greatest names of the millennium. The title of Newton's book is in reality a double *entendre*. Yes, Newton's friendships with each of these great men were unusual, but their friendships with each other rather than a bunch of sycophants were unusual as well. We become better tennis players by playing someone better than ourselves. Each of the friends—from Charles Lindbergh, who gave Ford his first airplane ride and during World War II was a Ford consultant, to Ford to Edison to Firestone to the naturalist John Burroughs—became better human beings for their friendships with each other. Their friendships grounded their humanity and helped them to be humble instead of demigods or devils that the press and the public would at one moment or another make them appear to be or want them to become. In many ways, acquiring fame in your own lifetime is a twentieth-century phenomenon. Certainly, famous people have existed since the dawn of time. However, the worldwide fame and recognition that these uncommon friends enjoyed was not only heady. It was stressful in the ages of mass media because almost everyone recognized you and most wanted a piece of you.

Ford retreated to his castle Fair Lane, Lindbergh withdrew to his Hawaii, and so forth. In their retreats, they sometimes embraced their worst selves. Isolation, whether on an island or in a castle surrounded by the foam of fame, in the long run is not good for the human soul. As society continues to embrace fame and isolate itself, perhaps the greatest lesson to be learned is the importance of friendship and partnership—whether in marriage, in work, or in play. These things are important if we are to remain on course with our lives and not brew a pot of bitter tea while we stew in our urban or exurban castles.

Fair Lane is such a pleasant-sounding place that more than forty establishments have adopted its name, although most spell it as one word. In naming his castle, Ford wanted to evoke the lane to the fairgrounds in County Cork, Ireland, from where his ancestors had come. Similar to the fair-goers of centuries past, Ford paved the lane of his life with many memorable times. Both the centennial fair in Philadelphia and the Columbian exposition in Chicago were predecessors to Ford's sharing his knowledge at the fairs of his era. The Michigan State Fair is the longest-running state fair in the nation. Ford probably attended it as a youth, and in his later years, he contributed some of its most memorable exhibits. (For example, in 1925, Ford's contribution was a miniature farm.) Ford's many achievements in transportation helped shrink the world and made the lane to the fair a fair lane every day.

Henry Ford spent his last months at Richmond Hill, Georgia. June Baylor and her husband Neil owned and lovingly maintained the 1840 Strathy Hall that Ford had restored. She shared a local saying as we walked down the beautiful aisle of live oak trees from the hall to the Ogeechee River docks:

> They say around here that live oak trees grow a hundred years, rest a hundred years, and die a hundred years.

Ford walked this earth and grew in wisdom and wealth for almost a century, and now perhaps his reputation will rest another hundred years. However, if humankind continues to exist, it is doubtful that Ford's reputation will ever die. The Charles Kettering [15-7] quote with which David Lewis in part closes his 1976 Ford biography rings true even today:

A thousand years from now when the names of Churchill and Roosevelt will be but mere footnotes in history, the name of Henry Ford will loom as the most significant of the age.

Kettering of General Motors fame was as close to a peer of Henry Ford as anyone could be, and he owed Ford nothing when he made that comment in 1943. Similar to Ford, Kettering had an intuitive and highly honed mind when it came to making world-class cars or setting up world-class hospitals or foundations with his wealth. My recent count of the number of references from Internet web sites related to the key words of Henry Ford, Churchill, and Roosevelt found that Ford is already rapidly outdistancing the most famous politicians of the age by a two-to-one count. It is not that Roosevelt's or Churchill's accomplishments were less important than what Ford did. We could rightly argue that the World War II victory was the most important event of this century. The point that Kettering makes with his 1943 comment is that Henry Ford was one of the most important figures not only for this century but for this millennium.

It would be presumptuous for anyone, including me, to argue that Ford was more or less important than any of a score of people in world history. Similar to the live oak aisle in Richmond Hill, the aisle of Ford's life took a century to grow, may take a century to rest, and another century to either die or for history to prepare his place as one of the great figures of world history. What is implicit in the fair judgment of Ford's life is that its many facets must be examined so that the light and sparkle of one or the dim failure of another does not put us in awe or completely in doubt of the life of Henry Ford. Perhaps Grace Prunk, one of Clara Ford's favorite nieces, said it best when she exclaimed:

> Uncle Henry was too much for all of us.

"Faith of Our Fathers" was Henry Ford's favorite hymn. The third verse is the concluding verse of this hymn that has stood the test of time and was found in many contemporary hymnals. I selected it as the most relevant verse because it reflects what Henry Ford "preached" and is the essence of a piece of age-old folk wisdom: Actions speak louder than words. Unfortunately, too many people have judged the life of Henry Ford on only a small number of his actions. These individuals are the poorer for this judgment because they will have missed a wonderful sermon on what to do and what not to do with wealth. Ford's perfection of the moving assembly line has worked to make us all wealthier. In attempting to sort the wheat kernels from the chaff of Ford's life, this book likewise attempts to make us wiser.

Faith of Our Fathers

Written by Frederick W. Faber (1814–1863)

Verse 3

Faith of our fathers we will love

Both friend and foe in all our strife:

And preach thee too as love knows how,

By kindly words and virtuous life:

Faith of our fathers, holy faith

We will be true to thee 'til death!

These hymns were among those used in the daily chapel services at Ford's Greenfield Village. They were remembered as Henry Ford's favorites by John Weeks in a letter to me dated June 20, 1986. From 1929 to approximately 1940, Mr. Weeks was the "director of music" at the Martha Mary Chapel, and his wife Catherine had also been a student at the Village schools.

- Abide With Me
- America the Beautiful
- In the Garden
- Blest Be the Tie That Binds
- Come to the Church in the Wildwood
- When They Ring the Golden Bells
- Memories of Galilee
- God Be With You
- Holy, Holy, Holy
- The Lily of the Valley
- I Need Thee Ever Hour
- Jesus Lover of My Soul
- Let the Lower Lights Be Burning
- Nearer My God to Thee
- Onward Christian Soldiers
- Rock of Ages
- Shall We Gather at the River
- Softly Now the Light of Day
- Sweet Hour of Prayer
- What A Friend We Have in Jesus

GREAT FORD STORIES

The following stories have been told many times by Henry Ford Estate volunteers and Fordophiles who recall with enthusiasm memorable encounters with Henry Ford. Wherever the person who experienced the encounter is the primary source, their name is noted. Otherwise, it is a story that has been woven into folklore passed down from those who first experienced it, told again and again.

Childhood, Youth, and Heroes

Henry Ford's first memory was that of a bird, probably a field sparrow. He said that he always remembered its song. In his autobiography *My Life and My Work,* Ford noted that the only time he used his corporation's power to pass legislation was to help pass the Migratory Bird Act of 1913. During this same time, Ford is listed as being on the board of directors of the Michigan Audubon Society. Following the death of one of Ford's heroes, the renowned literary naturalist John Burroughs, Ford forged a relationship with Jack Miner. Miner was a nearby Canadian who won the King George VI award for conservation. At Fair Lane, Henry Ford was once treed by a deer in rut. Ford never forgot his childhood love and sense of wonder about nature.

The Violin

Ford admired fiddlers, the "rock stars" of the nineteenth century. Although he learned to play the violin and had one of the greatest collections of violins in private possession, Henry Ford could never master what the best of the fiddlers of the "devil's box" could do: fiddle and dance at the same time.

Bruce Simpson, son of Ford's talented tractor engineer Howard Simpson, remembers Henry Ford as someone who not only loved the instrument but went out of his way to promote young people's mastery of it. Bruce recounts how Ford loaned him one of his Stradivarius violins on which to practice and even gave Bruce a quick bowing lesson. Bruce also remembers Ford putting the spotlight on a young Jewish-American violinist on one of the most popular radio programs of the day, the Ford Sunday Evening Hour.

Training and Renewal

At the Detroit shipyards, Ford learned from a master mechanic how to install engines in the great ferries and boats that plied the Great Lakes. This may have had as much to do with his success as his time spent tending the Westinghouse steam engine as part of a threshing ring.

Ford would put any college-trained engineer to an extra test. In Ford's library is a book entitled *Too Much College,* which accurately expresses his sentiments. How Martha Berry obtained millions of dollars from Ford to fund her college seems incomprehensible in retrospect. In the 1920s, however, the college was then known as the Berry Schools, and agricultural training there was much more prominent than it is today.

Racing was part of what made Ford successful, but he quickly found Barney Oldfield to take over the reins of the twin chariots, the race cars 999 and the Arrow.

Henry Ford enjoyed a good fire, indoors or outdoors. Henry is in the back with Clara behind him. John Burroughs, Ford's naturalist friend, is seated in the front near the center. (Photograph from the Collections of Henry Ford Museum & Greenfield Village)

Ford and Money

Billy Smith of Birmingham, Alabama, recalls a story from his student days at Berry College. Henry Ford was walking through a construction zone when he heard one ditch digger say to the other, "What I wouldn't give to just have the money Ford is carrying in his pants." Ford stopped and opened all his pockets and made the ditch digger the beneficiary of thirty-seven cents.

At Richmond Hill, Clara Ford gave their German-American maid Rosa Buhler twenty-five cents to go into town and buy a certain piece of fabric. In Henry Ford's presence, Clara directed Rosa not to pay more than that amount for the fabric. In town, Rosa found the fabric Clara wanted, but the price was forty-two cents. She paid the difference from her own purse. When Rosa returned, Henry Ford asked Rosa in German how much she had to pay, not wanting to betray her generosity at the expense of irritating his penny-wise wife. Afterward, Rosa asked Mr. Ford how he had learned German. He responded that his father used to hire summer help who were recent German immigrants.

In Ireland, Ford was approached to make a donation of five thousand pounds for the construction of a new hospital, which he pledged on the spot. The next day, the newspaper lauded Henry Ford's donation of fifty thousand pounds. The embarrassed fundraisers came to apologize for the error, whereupon Ford said he would increase his pledge if they promised to carve over the main entrance the words: "I came among you, and you took me in." It was a double *entendre* of the truest kind.

Thomas Edison least enjoyed the publicity gathered by the camping trips of the Four Vagabonds—Harvey Firestone, John Burroughs, Henry Ford, and Thomas Edison. Firestone and Ford seemed to enjoy it, to a point. Firestone used the trips to demonstrate the ruggedness of his tires, whereas Ford relished the outdoor life and the manifest destiny of how the car/recreational vehicle generation should be born to enjoy in comfort all of God's creation. On one such trip, a skeptical farmer refused to believe Henry Ford's introduction of Edison, Firestone, and himself. The farmer looked at the fourth vagabond, John Burroughs, who had a long white beard, and told Ford, "and I suppose that guy with the beard is Santa Claus?"

Adult Ford Heroes

During the 1934 World Series between the St. Louis Cardinals and the Detroit Tigers, Henry Ford invited to Fair Lane the Cardinals' great wisecracking pitcher, Dizzy Dean. At the front door, Dean is reported to have said, "Mr. Ford, I am honored to meet you, but I have to tell you that I am going to make pussycats out of your Tigers." Dizzy Dean did just that, teaming with his brother Paul to win all four games. However, in 1935 when the Tigers won the World Series, Henry Ford in thanks gave each Tiger a new car.

Helping the Handicapped

The following story is similar to one I have heard dozens of times in multiple places associated with Henry Ford. Ruth Chavey of Dearborn, Michigan, is now in her nineties, but she shared that her handicapped husband was on crutches during part of the Depression. Riding with him on Ford Road one day, they had stopped to watch the deer of Fair Lane. Henry Ford himself walked over to them and asked Ruth what was wrong with her husband. Because it was the Depression era and the Chaveys could not afford a doctor, Ruther responded that she did not know. Henry Ford took their name and address, and he said his driver would come by to have her young husband treated by Ford's personal physician.

Church Attendance

Ed Cushman, a former vice president of American Motors and later of Wayne State University, attended the same church and Dearborn social functions as the Fords did. At Christ Episcopal Church, Cushman remembers that Ford told him he often was not at church because he hated the social climbers who would use religious occasions to advance themselves in one way or another. Cushman shared his life-long impression of Ford and other extremely creative people. There was, he said, an aura of energy and power that you could not touch but you certainly could feel. When Cushman spoke of Ford, he would lay down his cigar and pause in thoughtful silence. Through the years, Cushman bore a sense of honor at having worked, talked, and walked with such a man as Henry Ford.

An Apple a Day

Louie Hagopian, a gardener for the Fords, recalls how Henry Ford one day found Hagopian standing by the root cellar, where Henry Ford stored his root crops and apples. Hagopian had one apple ready to eat and one bulging from the back pocket of his overalls. Ford simply said, "One apple is okay, but two you'll have to work for."

Richmond Hill, Georgia

Now the site of a major upscale real estate development, many of the nineteenth century structures Ford saved and restored still exist to view and enjoy. Also remaining are some twentieth-century additions, including a little girl's handprints pressed into concrete in Ford's yacht basin. The prints belong to Charlotte Ford, Henry's great-granddaughter, who must have been visiting when the concrete was poured. Her father, Henry II, had lit the blast furnaces of the mighty Rouge plant as an approving grandfather watched, and it was probably the elder Henry Ford who encouraged his great-granddaughter to leave her ceremonial mark as well. The Rouge steel operation has since been sold. Perhaps the development of Henry Ford's great social experiment and retreat will destroy Charlotte's handprints. As with her father lighting the blast furnace, this describes how Ford always sought to bring youth to the forefront.

Fair Lane

Henry and Clara Ford actually did whistle to each other at Fair Lane, using bird calls to find one another in the enormous house. Whether they whistled the warble of the Jenny wren or the field sparrow is not remembered, but both loved birds all their lives.

Christmas at Fair Lane originally was celebrated in the Field Room, with its rustic walls and massive fieldstone fireplace. Grace Prunk, Clara's beloved niece, remembers that the Christmas tree was always to the right of the fireplace, with a simple linen tablecloth wrapped around the base. Francis ImOberstag, another favorite niece from Clara's Bryant side of the family, remembers that even in his fifties, Henry Ford had a penchant for taking anything mechanical apart and that she was cautioned accordingly. If she were not vigilant, Ford would take apart her new Christmas toys to satisfy his engineer's curiosity that had not changed since his childhood. Except for the basement tree and a tree decorated for the birds outdoors, the Fords did not really decorate for Christmas, as was the custom of their contemporaries. John McIntyre, a long-term gardener, recalled an umbrella stand stacked with poinsettias in the main entrance hall and poinsettias by the dozens in the pool room, waiting to be shipped as Christmas gifts.

Ford's first restoration was that of the historic farmstead on which he was raised, a little more than a mile away from Fair Lane. He began this work in 1919 and kept a watchful eye on the project in the years that followed. One day, Ford was riding his bicycle and saw a group of youths by the farm. The girls remained respectfully behind the fence, while the boys clambered over the fence to peer in the windows. Ford chased off the boys, but he gave the girls a personal inside-and-outside tour of his homestead.

John H. Williams, Fair Lane's houseman from 1922 to 1950, related the following account. Clara Ford had a little motorboat called *Callie B.*, and she would take the children for rides in it. One day as Clara was preparing to go for a ride, Henry Ford approached Williams and said, "John, you watch Mrs. Ford out there in the river, and if anything goes wrong, you jump in and save her." Williams later related, "I said, 'Yes, Mr. Ford.' But I couldn't swim a stroke."

Greatest Compliment to Henry Ford

Thomas Edison said that Henry Ford's foresight was so long, it sagged in the middle.

Ford's most farsighted publication was, "The Little White Slaver," an early anti-smoking pamphlet.

Ford's Greatest Achievement

Ford's outstanding achievements include the Model T, historic restoration, wildlife preservation, historic preservation, the V-8 engine cast in a single block, the assembly line, and his work with soybeans. In the end, of what was Henry Ford most proud?

There would be many things from which to choose, but Ford himself indicated his work with the soybean was his most important. In 1996, William Shurtleff and Akiko Aoyagi published 439 works that document Ford's work with the soybean. The anthology is titled *Henry Ford and His Researchers' Work with Soybeans, Soyfoods, and Chemurgy: Bibliography and Sourcebook, 1921–1996*. As an example, the authors state:

> Indeed a strong case can be made that Henry Ford and his coworkers played the pioneer role in developing American-style soyfoods and introducing them in a big way to America. In so doing, they set the stage for the rapid rise of soyfood consumption among typical Americans that began in a small way during World War II, and in a big way starting in the 1970s and continuing into the 1990s.

The Consequences of Youthful Trespass at Fair Lane

Grey-haired Dearborn residents today remember in their youth being accosted by Mr. Ford himself when they trespassed on Ford's extensive holdings. The outcome of the encounter was a ride back to the village, with the offer of a weed sandwich from the George Washington Carver Laboratory on Michigan Avenue.

Henry Ford enjoyed many great successes and embraced many celebrated and uncelebrated failures. Here, Clem Glotzhober is vacuuming dandelion fluff in the center of Southfield Road which, even in the 1940s, was a busy thoroughfare. Ford was working with Dr. George Washington Carver of Tuskegee Institute to find uses for weeds. In possibly his "wildest" idea, Ford hoped that the dandelion fluff could be a wartime substitute for the tropical kapok plant used in life jackets. Glotzhober did not feel nearly the embarrassment felt by Howard Simpson, Ford's tractor engineer, when Ford brought tractor manufacturers to see a one-wheeled tractor attempt to defy the laws of physics. There was only stunned silence. (Photograph from the Collection of Richard Folsom, President, Henry Ford Heritage Association)

Henry Ford may not have had all the facts we know today, but history has proven him correct. Ford's campaign against smoking was a pioneering effort in the war with cigarettes. (Photograph from the Collections of Henry Ford Museum & Greenfield Village)

Ford and His Grandchildren

One year at the annual Dearborn Historical Society, I was honored to sit next to a veteran Ford pilot. He recalled how he had buzzed Clara Ford in his Ford Tri-motor one day. When he landed, it did not take long before he received the expected call from Clara Ford, who was not used to having her tranquility disturbed. The pilot silenced Mrs. Ford with only a few words because Henry Ford had been at the airport with his grandchildren, driving his Ford across the path of incoming planes and causing them to pull up to avoid a collision. The pilot never saw Henry Ford do such a foolish thing again. What was Henry Ford doing? Put this instance together with how he tried to steel other young men, and we could easily conclude that Ford wanted his grandchildren to be irreverent to existing authority or convention. In looking over the lives of the two famous Henry's, grandson Henry Ford II, who was riding in the car that day, may have been more like his grandfather than either ever acknowledged. Both made decisions their way because their name was on the company.

On the ninetieth anniversary of Ford Motor Company, William Clay Ford, the last living grandson of Henry and Clara, recalled how his grandfather taught him to drive when he was only ten years old. Once a policeman stopped them and asked first for William's driver's license and then for his grandfather's, neither of whom had one. At this point, the policeman did a smart thing. He called Grandmother Clara and, as with the instance at the airport, that was the end of the story.

Floyd Apple, who worked as a boiler operator at Fair Lane power-house from 1925 to 1950, recalls Clara bringing her granddaughter Josephine Ford to the powerhouse to see how the ice machine worked. Despite Clara's powerhouse tutelage, Josephine became known for her ever-changing gardens rather than an interest in machines.

Architectural Details

Fair Lane was designed by two different sets of architects. Ford had fired the first architect and hired a second, after paying a tidy sum to break the initial contract. One detail that remained virtually the same at Fair Lane is the log cabin room or Field Room, which appears in the early as well as the constructed designs. Evidently, Ford wanted a rustic cabin-like room conveniently located in the basement of his residence for square-dancing, hearthside cooking, and reminiscing with his Four Vagabond friends. Likenesses of the friends were carved in wood and placed as bracket figures on their sides in the four corners of the main part of the room. In later years, the room became little

used by Ford, and the bracket figures were sold. Perhaps the mist of the past was too heavy for Ford in this room. He was much more sentimental than would be conveyed by our first impression of this mechanic from Dearborn. All of Ford's camping friends died years, even decades, before Ford died. Perhaps selling the bracket figures, which have since been reproduced based on the originals that are now in Texas, was a way for Ford to avoid such reminders of his own mortality. Jim Newton recalled his mission to tell Ford directly of Harvey Firestone's death. According to Newton, on the long walk that followed the sharing of the sad news, Ford was quite moved.[A-1] The architect of record, William Van Tine, wrote that the Field Room captured the true heart of the owner. In later years, it may well have become a heartbreaking reminder of his lost friends. The fact that the room is one of the few features (excluding the swimming pool) retained from the first plans for Fair Lane implies its special significance to Ford.

Preserving the Social Memory of the Land

The well on the old Black farm was never filled by Ford. Instead, the hand-laid stones became the centerpiece of the Fords' bleaching yard or outdoor clothes-hanging area. After Monday's wash was taken indoors, the place became a pleasant garden that continues to greet visitors to the Estate today. The black locust trees of Locust Lane, which were part of the original Black farm, also were left standing to preserve the memory of the land. Today, they are in decline, although locust can live well beyond the century mark. The reason is that these locust trees were not vintage 1915, but were planted in the nineteenth century by members of the Black family who dug the well and constructed the nearby root cellar that Ford retained and used to store his apples.

The Architectural Record of Henry Ford

Abraham Lincoln has been quoted as saying, "Never switch horses in the middle of the stream." The results can be disastrous. The first architectural firm to design Fair Lane, Von Holst and Fyfe of Chicago, assigned the aspiring Marion Mahoney to design Fair Lane. Numerous rumors abound as to why her striking Prairie School design was not built. However, the one that makes some sense is that Clara and probably Henry did not like the *avant-garde* triangular-shaped fireplace in the main central living room. The traditional fireplace that is there today is rather expensive, not only in terms of the six-figure contract settlement Ford made with the original architects, but also because of the cost to the design integrity of the home in which Clara and Henry Ford lived for more than three decades. The final version of the Fords' home has one foot in the nineteenth century and one foot in the twentieth century, as did the Fords themselves. The Fords never rehired the final architect, William Van Tine, who had opened a Detroit office in anticipation of a boon in business that never materialized. They grew vines over the house, which is what Frank Lloyd Wright recommended as the only solution when an architect makes a mistake. The Fords came to love Fair Lane more for its gardens, setting, and interiors, although they turned to Albert Kahn to do their first remodeling of the first-floor area. Kahn was known more for his industrial buildings, which he designed for Ford and which became world-class innovations. In Georgia, in Massachusetts, at the Dearborn Inn, and at his many restorations, Ford left an architectural record of excellence, albeit of the traditional kind. The only innovation seemed to be Ford's penchant for exhibiting the power that made things work. Even at Fair Lane's powerhouse, the path that leads to Edison's cornerstone awkwardly hugs the boiler and wheel room walls where Ford entices visitors to peer in the windows to see raw power at work—the basis of our power-hungry civilization. In some ways, Ford never lost his pre-Titanic mindset. Industrial power was the Archimedean lever with which people could move the world. Ford wanted the world to know that fact, whether as a guest at Fair Lane or as a tourist at Greenfield Village or one of his twenty village industries.

Some say the watch inspired Henry Ford to create the moving assembly line. I believe the threshing disassembly line of Ford's childhood, which also moved, was a likely inspiration also. Ford loved to tinker with watches, and engineers on the top floor of the powerhouse knew he would stop by their drafting boards and then move to the south side of the Experimental Room to tinker with watches. (Photograph from the Collections of the Henry Ford Estate, the University of Michigan–Dearborn, donated by Wilbur Donaldson)

HIBENJOBILL

This miniature steam engine and threshing set was named after the four Ford grandchildren: Henry, Benson, Josephine, and William Clay. Henry Ford had this equipment made especially for the 1924 Michigan State Fair. A complete miniature farm also was made for the 1924 exhibit. From the time HIBENJOBILL was returned to Fair Lane, there is extensive film footage of Ford's grandchildren threshing with the equipment, demonstrating his view of learning. Ford felt that learning should be "hands on" and realistic, so that you feel the itch of the grain as well as the product of teamwork. Ford's experience working in a threshing ring was undoubtedly good training for himself in creating and managing the assembly line. Thus, Ford wanted children to experience and learn from the same. Ford was an accomplished race car driver, ice skater, and dancer—all individual accomplishments. The teamwork needed to build a company into one of the largest in the world was something that Ford, his grandchildren, and hundreds more learned at the Fair and later at Greenfield Village. Threshing grain was a disassembly process that required teamwork from start to finish.

Healthy Lifestyle

Carl Post was a powerhouse operator and later volunteered as a guide at the Estate for many years. Although he knew better than to smoke on the job, Post did chew tobacco—until Henry Ford would happen by, of course. Post told Mike Skinner, a long-time guide at the Estate, that he probably swallowed more than twenty pounds of tobacco in his years of service. Ford, who disliked tobacco in all forms, was never the wiser.

Perhaps the Fords' good health was bolstered by their joyful appreciation of all four seasons. They usually left Michigan for their winter homes in late winter, first to Ft. Myers and then to Georgia, at Richmond Hill. For Henry Ford, January in Michigan meant the opportunity to ice skate on his specially built pond. Ford ice skated well past his sixties, and from historic film footage, he seemed to enjoy it. Ice skating for Ford resembled dancing on ice, and he was good, if not excellent, at both. In the summer, Ford would footrace youngsters half his age and faithfully ride his bike. However, similar to many natives of Michigan, Ford loved all four seasons. In some ways, winter was almost preferred because you could work and play hard and long without becoming drenched in sweat. February was for maple sugaring in Ford's extensive sugar bush. On the other hand, March meant mud and cold rain, making a Georgia or Florida sun truly appreciated.

Homefront War Preparations

In World War I, Clara packed apples from the Fords' extensive orchards and sent them to England. Henry Ford sent his first five thousand Fordson tractors to England to replace horses that had been sent to the front.

Dick Folsom, the first president of the Henry Ford Heritage Association, recalls this story told by Floyd Apple, a boiler operator at Fair Lane from 1925 to 1950. The day after the bombing of Pearl Harbor in 1941, Henry Ford asked Apple, "How much dirt do we have over the tunnel [a one-hundred-yard underground connection between the main house and powerhouse]?" Ford told Apple to get a tape, and together they measured it as being fourteen feet. Ford later commented to Apple in the powerhouse that the tunnel would make a good bomb shelter "…if we ever get in trouble over here."

Another Floyd Apple story, perhaps from the same period, involves Clara Ford, who ran from her garden, yelling, "Fireman, fireman!" There was no fire—there was a snake in the garden, and Clara Ford wanted Apple to kill it with his shovel. Dick Folsom, who heard this story and many more from Ford estate workers, asked Apple if he killed it. Apple said he found the snake, picked it up behind the head, and gave it a verbal warning that Mrs. Ford was after its life. Then, he threw it in the brush. Today, many snakes can be found at Fair Lane, but the garters, as the one Floyd picked up and lectured, are harmless—unless you are an insect, mouse, or garden pest.

Favorite Model T Story

Did you hear about the man who wanted to be buried with his Model T? No? Well, his Model T had gotten him out of every hole into which he ever fell.

Henry Ford, Practical Joker

Dall Hutchinson, one of Henry Ford's faithful young students and a former employee at Greenfield Village, recalls the following story. We all have our vanity, and Ford was no exception. With celebrities such as Will Rogers visiting him, a "little planned trick" was devised to convince the visitor of Henry Ford's great eyesight, particularly when Ford was in his mid-seventies with eyesight not as keen as it was in prior years. Ford would ask if either Wilson (his driver) or Hutchinson had a penny. Then, both Ford and Rogers might look at it to see if they could read the date on the penny. Rogers said he felt fortunate even to be able to see the penny; however, Ford would take the penny from him and exclaim, "Oh, yes, 1913—is that right?" Then Ford would hand the penny to Hutchinson or Wilson, who would quickly say, "Yes, that's right, Mr. Ford" before putting away the penny for the next visitor. The visitor would leave, saying, "Gee, that Mr. Ford certainly does have good eyesight for his age!"

Hutchinson also shared another tale. On another occasion, Henry Ford realized that constant bickering had been occurring between two middle-management employees—one at Greenfield Village and the other in the museum. Ford said, "Let's give them a little lesson. I'll tell each one to go fire the other, and we will watch what happens." You can imagine the scene on the village green as the two individuals tried to "fire" each other, with neither leaving the premises!

Henry Ford's Motto

Henry Ford's motto was "Help the other fella." Jack Miner, Henry's naturalist friend from Canada, inscribed his autobiography to Henry Ford with these words on the inside front cover:

> You can do all you can for the other fellow, but it is a failure unless he himself is willing to get up in the morning."

Jack Miner was Henry Ford's friend for 30 years. Miner was recipient of the Order of the British Empire from King George VI in 1943 for "the greatest achievement in conservation in the British Empire."

BIBLIOGRAPHY

Books

Aird, Hazel B., and Ruddiman, Catherine, *Henry Ford: Boy With Ideas*. The Bobbs-Merrill Company, New York, 1960.

Bassett, Beth Dawkins, *Berry College: Building Upon the Miracle*. Corporate Stories, Ltd., Atlanta, 1996.

Bray, Mayfield, *Guide to the Ford Film Collection*. The National Archives, Washington, DC, 1970.

Brunk, Thomas W., *Leonard B. Willeke: Excellence in Architecture and Design*. University of Detroit Press, Detroit, 1986.

Bryan, Ford, *Beyond the Model T: The Other Ventures of Henry Ford*. Wayne State University Press, Detroit, 1990.

Bryan, Ford, *Henry's Lieutenants*. Wayne State University Press, Detroit, 1993.

Ford, Henry, with Crowther, Samuel, *My Life and My Work*, Garden City Publishing Co., Garden City, NY, 1927.

Ford, Henry, *My Philosophy of Industry; An Authorized Interview by Fay Leon Faroute*. Coward-McCann, Inc., New York, 1929.

Garfield, Curtis F., and Ridley, Alison R., *Henry Ford's Boys: The Story of the Wayside Inn Boys School*. Porcupine Enterprises, Sudbury, MA, 1998.

Henry Ford Hospital, *Information for Patients*, pamphlet, circa 1930.

Josephson, Matthew, *Edison: A Biography*. John Wiley & Sons, New York, 1959.

Kremer, Gary R., *George Washington Carver: In His Own Words*. University of Missouri Press, Columbia, MO, 1987.

Lacey, Robert, *Ford, the Men and the Machine*. Little Brown and Company, Boston-Toronto, 1986.

Leffingwell, Randy, *Ford Farm Tractors*. MBI Publishing Company, Osceola, WI, 1998.

Lewis, David L., *The Public Image of Henry Ford*. Wayne State University Press, Detroit, 1986.

Long, Franklin Leslie, and Long, Lucy Bunce, *The Henry Ford Era at Richmond Hill, Georgia*. Darien Printing & Graphics, Darien, GA, 1998.

McNairn, William and Marjorie, *Quotations from the Unusual Henry Ford*. Quotamus Press, Redondo Beach, CA, 1978.

Moreland, Faye Witt, *Green Fields and Fairer Lanes: Music in the Life of Henry Ford*. Five Star Publishers, Tupelo, MO, 1969.

Nevins, Allan, and Hill, Frank Ernest, *Ford: Expansion and Challenge, 1915–1933*. Charles Scribner's Sons, New York, 1957.

Newton, James, *Uncommon Friends: Life with Thomas Edison, Henry Ford, Harvey Firestone, Alexis Carrel, and Charles Lindbergh.* Harcourt Brace Jovanovich, San Diego, 1987.

Painter, Patricia Scollard, *Henry Ford Hospital: The First 75 Years.* Henry Ford Health System, Detroit, 1997.

Sorenson, Charles, with Williamson, Samuel T., *Forty Years with Ford,* Norton and Co., New York, 1956.

Twork, Eva O'Neal, *Henry Ford and Benjamin B. Lovett: The Dancing Billionaire and the Dance Master.* Harlo Press, Detroit, 1982.

Upward, Geoffrey C., *A Home for Our Heritage: The Building and Growth of Greenfield Village and Henry Ford Museum, 1929–1979.* The Henry Ford Museum Press, Dearborn, 1979.

Zia, Z.K., and Chen, W.C., *Henry Ford: His Struggle.* Christian Literature Society, Shanghai, 1929.

Oral Histories

Apple, Floyd. Taken by Dick Folsom. From the Collections of Henry Ford Museum and Greenfield Village. Floyd Apple worked at the powerhouse of Fair Lane from 1925 to 1950. In addition to this formal oral history, I had many conversations with Floyd Apple about his life with the Fords.

Avery, W.G. W.G. Avery was interviewed by me. He worked for Ford as a young man and then enjoyed a successful career in the truck body manufacturing business in Jackson, Mississippi. He appeared outside the garage of Fair Lane one summer day in his chauffeur-driven Cadillac. Avery's story so impressed Bruno Gluski, who was then the facilities engineer for the University of Michigan–Dearborn, that Gluski summoned me. Avery then repeated his stories of the early days at the powerhouse and garage, circa 1918 to 1920.

Bacon, Irving. From the Collections of Henry Ford Museum and Greenfield Village. Bacon was the artist of the Fords, including the creation of Ford's 1941 heroic bust now in the Estate Visitor Center.

Buhler, Rosa, and Thompson, J.D. From the Collections of Henry Ford Museum and Greenfield Village. Rosa Buhler and Mr. J.D. Thompson were long-time servants of the Fords at Fair Lane.

Caldwell, Alfred. Henry Ford Estate Video Collection. Speech to the First Landscape Institute at the Clearing on Jens Jensen, 1994. Caldwell, who was in his nineties but continued to teach at the Illinois Institute of Technology, had vibrant memories of Jens Jensen and Fair Lane. I stayed in the same cabin with Caldwell and Jensen's grandson, and we had many interesting conversations about Jensen and the Fords.

Davis, Clem. From the Collections of Henry Ford Museum and Greenfield Village. In addition to this formal oral history, the story in the text of the weight falling through the bottom of the clock was shared with me by the Eurich family, who purchased the clock from Clem Davis and later donated it to the Henry Ford Museum. The Museum has since returned the clock to the Estate, and it again stands in its historic place.

De Caluwe, Alfons. From the Collections of Henry Ford Museum and Greenfield Village. Alfons De Caluwe was a long-time head gardener at Fair Lane.

Donaldson, Wilbur. Wilbur Donaldson was a driver for Henry Ford in the 1930s, and I interviewed Donaldson in 1996.

Farkas, Eugene. "The Reminiscences of Mr. E.J. Farkas." From the Collections of Henry Ford Museum and Greenfield Village. Eugene Farkas was the engineer who worked for Henry Ford in the top floor of the Experimental Room. Farkas took over the X engine project and worked on tractor design and the Model A, not only at the Estate but at other Ford laboratories as well.

Glotzhober, Clem. "Some of My Experiences with Henry Ford," unpublished manuscript detailing Clem Glotzhober's interactions with Henry Ford dating back to 1929 and Glotzhober's work during the 1940s as a botanist at the George Washington Carver Laboratory.

Hicks, Harold. From the Collections of Henry Ford Museum and Greenfield Village, Vols. I–IV. Harold Hicks was an engineer who worked for Ford. He began the X engine project in 1919 to develop the replacement engine for the Model T.

Liebold, E.G. From the Collections of Henry Ford Museum and Greenfield Village. E.G. Liebold was Ford's long-time personal secretary.

Liimatainen, Kathryn. I interviewed Kathryn Liimatainen by telephone after her recent visit to the bungalow in Pequaming, MI. She and her brothers had attended Ford's Pequaming High School. Both brothers eventually obtained doctorate degrees, but both treasured Ford's educational philosophy of training the hands as well as the head. Kathryn worked as a cook at the bungalow when Ford visited. She described Ford's visits as those of a perfect plain-speaking gentleman who liked to teach children how to dance. According to Kathryn, Ford was "such a nice man" who came into the kitchen to greet the help and see the kitchen.

Long, Leslie and Lucy. Interview with me at the Henry Ford Estate on June 7, 1996.

Newton, Jim. Informal telephone conversations and meetings from 1990 to 1996, during which Ford and Newton's book, *Uncommon Friends*, were discussed.

Priebe, Harold, son of the former mayor of Fordson. Interviewed October 16, 1996 by me and Joel Hurley, who was a Henry Ford Estate research archivist assistant.

Prunk, Grace. Henry Ford Estate Oral History Archives. Grace Prunk was one of Clara Ford's nieces who traveled with and visited the Fords frequently.

Sheldrick, Mr. L.S. "The Reminiscences of Mr. L.S. Sheldrick." From the Collections of Henry Ford Museum and Greenfield Village. Larry Sheldrick was a former Ford Motor Company engineer.

Simpson, Howard. "The Reminiscences of Mr. and Mrs. Howard Simpson." From the Collections of Henry Ford Museum and Greenfield Village, February 1956. Howard Simpson was Ford's head tractor engineer and inventor.

Stout, Otto, Informal interview by me, circa 1985, and numerous conversations since then concerning Stout's trips down the river by raft to meet his friend, Henry Ford.

Other Resources

The Congressional Record, Sixty-Third Congress, Third Session, March 3, 1915, Vol. 5, Part 5, pp. 5470–5471.

"The Engine That Never Was," *Automotive Topics*, June–July, 1956.

Ruddiman, Edsel. Ford Archives: Ford correspondence, June 23, 1926.

Wren, Daniel A., and Greenwood, Ronald G., "Business Leaders: A Historical Sketch of Henry Ford." *The Journal of Leadership Studies*, Vol. 5, No. 3, 1998, pp. 72–79.

Final Comment on the Sources for This Book

Each year, each month, and each week—in fact, almost daily—another bit of historical reminiscence comes through Fair Lane as would a spring breeze. People's lives were so touched by Henry Ford—from Florida to the Keewenaw Bay of Lake Superior—that together they form a spring breeze that sweeps away the conclusion that Henry Ford was a closet Fascist who used his wealth to manipulate taste along lines he thought healthy. Whether biographers, the media, or other people are waiting to form their own conclusions about who were the significant people of this century, my observation has been that the more distant and less familiar people are with Henry Ford's life and work, the more harsh their judgment.

Not only do so many memories portray positive accolades of Henry Ford, but again and again it is the same set of accolades of which they speak. This suggests that Henry Ford was a decent human being who made mistakes but left a legacy. That legacy will stretch as far as Ford's greatest peer, Charles Kettering, in 1943 said it would: "A thousand years from now, when the Churchills and Roosevelts are but footnotes in history, Henry Ford will loom as the most significant figure of our age."

NOTES

Introduction

i.   Zia, Z.K., and Chen, W.C., *Henry Ford: His Struggle*. Christian Literature Society, Shanghai, 1929.

ii.   Told to me at the January 7, 1997, meeting of the Richmond Hill Historical Society, Richmond Hill, Georgia, by Marjorie Young.

iii.   Interview of H.G. Cooper in Darien, Georgia, on January 14, 1997, by me and John Berger.

iv.   McNairn, William and Marjorie, *Quotations from the Unusual Henry Ford*. Quotamus Press, Redondo Beach, CA, 1978, p. 97.

v.   Camp Legion Program, as shown to me by Lester Twork in 1997.

vi.   Interview of H.G. Cooper, *op. cit.*

Chapter 1—Cornerstones

1-1.   Ruskin, John, "The Builders," found in Barrows, Marjorie, *One Thousand Beautiful Things*, Spencer Press, New York, 1948.

1-2.   Ford, Henry, *My Life and Work*. Garden City Publishing, New York, 1927, p. 281.

1-3.   A circa-1930 poster of a farmer/citizen standing with one foot in a miniature town and one foot in the field hangs in the Archives of the Henry Ford Museum and Greenfield Village in Dearborn, Michigan, filed as #P.D. 1265, Just in Time Online photo collection.

1-4.   W.G. Avery stopped by Fair Lane unexpectedly in his chauffeur-driven Cadillac, circa 1990. Avery was interviewed by me and Bruno Gluski, P.E., of the campus plant department, about his years from 1918 to 1920 when he shuttled Ford's Model T back to the garage because Ford walked home. In later years, Avery founded W.G. Body Works in Jackson, Mississippi.

1-5.   "The Reminiscences of Mr. E.J. Farkas," Vol. II, June, 1952, pp. 133 and 171. From the Collections of Henry Ford Museum and Greenfield Village, Dearborn, MI.

1-6.   *Ibid.*, pp. 114 and 131–134.

1-7.   Henry Ford Museum Archives, Accession No. 1, Box 180-2, pp. 1–2.

1-8.   "The Reminiscences of John McIntyre." From the Collections of Henry Ford Museum and Greenfield Village.

1-9.   Village Industries poster, *op. cit.*

Chapter 2–Fair Lane's Garage

2-1.   "The Reminiscences of Floyd Apple," 1954. From the Collections of Henry Ford Museum and Greenfield Village.

2-2.   "The Reminiscences of Harold Hicks," Vol. I, pp. 34–37. From the Collections of Henry Ford Museum and Greenfield Village.

2-3.   Fahnestock, Murray, "The Engine that Never Was," *Automotive Topics*, June–July, 1956, Society of Automotive Engineers, pp. 20–21.

2-4.   Farkas and Hicks oral reminiscences, *op. cit.*

Chapter 3–Fair Lane: The Residence

3-1.   Clark, Glenn, *The Man Who Talks with the Flowers; The Intimate Life Story of Dr. George Washington Carver*, Macalaster Park Publishing, St. Paul, MN, 1939.

3-2.   Nevins, Allan, and Hill, Frank Ernest, *Ford: Expansion and Challenge, 1915–1933*. Charles Scribner's Sons, New York, 1957, p. 320.

3-3.   Conversations with numerous Ford associates and friends, including Wilbur Donaldson, retired personal driver for Ford and son of a long-time *Dearborn Independent* staff member; Grace Prunk, niece of Clara Ford; and Margaret Fleischauer, daughter of the Rabbi Leo Franklin. All contributed to this composite vignette on Ford's anti-Semitism.

3-4.   The Boston-Edison neighborhood is now one of the largest residential National Historic Districts in the country. It was the place to live in Detroit during the post-turn-of-the-century boom.

3-5.   In grade school, John Burroughs had been Jay Gould's schoolmate.

3-6.   "The Reminiscences of John Williams." From the Collections of Henry Ford Museum and Greenfield Village.

3-7.   Henry Ford, *op. cit.*, p. 170.

3-8.   "The Reminiscences of Grace Prunk." Henry Ford Estate Oral History Archives.

3-9.   A medieval term, meaning "without profit."

3-10.   Sorenson, Charles, *My Forty Years with Ford*, W.W. Norton, New York, 1956, p. 271.

3-11.   Despite these publications, Ford never discriminated against the hiring of Jewish people or members of any other race.

Chapter 5–The Upper Peninsula and the Huron Mountain Club

5-1.   This estimate was based on 1920 dollars. From a lecture by Professor David Lewis, "Henry Ford, An Historical Perspective." University of Michigan Press, Ann Arbor, MI, 1998.

5-2.   Rhydholm, Fred C., *Superior Heartland*. Braun-Brumfield, Ann Arbor, MI, 1989, p. 514.

5-3.   Ford Motor Company was losing millions at the time, and the challenge for Henry Ford II was to make the company profitable again.

Chapter 7–Richmond Hill, Georgia: Ford's Last Great Vision

7-1.   Nevins, Allan, *Ford: The Times, The Man, The Company*. Charles Scribner's Sons, New York, 1954, p. 167. Edison's comment referred specifically to Ford's development of a working gasoline-powered engine.

7-2.   "Hermitage Mansion Near Savannah Bought by Ford." *Pembroke Journal*, Pembroke, GA, March 8, 1935.

7-3   Riddle, Lyn, "There's a Ford in Its Past and a Resort in Its Future." *New York Times*, Sunday, June 14, 1998.

7-4.   *Ibid.*

Chapter 9–Henry Ford, Home Builder

9-1.   Wilbur Donaldson oral reminiscences to me in 1997.

Chapter 11–Henry Ford, Pioneer Preservationist

11-1.   Upward, Geoffrey C., *A Home for Our Heritage*, The Edison Institute, Dearborn, MI, 1979, p. 2.

Chapter 12–Henry Ford at Play

12-1.   *Peoria Journal Star*, Sunday, April 1, 1951.

12-2.   A Michigan law in the 1870s stated that as long as a log could float down a stream, a fence could not be run across the stream.

12-3.   Floyd Apple oral reminiscences, *op. cit.*

Chapter 14–Memories of Mr. Ford's Passing

14-1.   Floyd Apple oral reminiscences, *op. cit.*

14-2.   Wilbur Donaldson, conversation with me, *op. cit.*

Chapter 15–Ebb Power: The Ford Legacy in the Balance

15-1.   In the next U.A.W. contract following Henry Ford's death, the right to smoke on the job was "won" again. Decades later, that "enlightened policy" was replaced with Henry Ford's nonsmoking policy of decades previous.

15-2.   "Henry Ford," *Journal of Negro History*, 32, July 1947, p. 400.

15-3.   In 1995, I spoke with Rabbi Leo Franklin's great-grandson, a rabbi from California, who was touring the Henry Ford Estate, and later his mother and grandmother, all of whom shared similar interesting and somewhat surprising remembrances of Rabbi Franklin and Henry Ford. Ford was many things good and bad in his complex and controversial life. However, for all the negative hype about Ford, as a neighbor and a friend, he was known and appreciated for his many acts of understanding and even humble kindness, regardless of age, sex, or race.

15-4.   National Inventors Hall of Fame, World Wide Web site: http://www.invent.org/book/book-text/43.html.

15-5.   National Aviation Hall of Fame, World Wide Web site: http://www.nationalaviation.org.

15-6.   Leffingwell, Randy, *Ford Farm Tractors*. MBI Publishing Company, Osceola, 1998. p. 127.

15-7. Charles Kettering was a vice president of General Motors, as well as the inventor of the electric starter, which Ford added to his Model T.

Appendix–Great Ford Stories

A-1. Harvey Firestone had been one of Ford's oldest and closest friends. Jim Newton had been Firestone's valued vice-president and protégé. Jim had quit his job as part of a commitment to a renewal of his Christian faith, which he shared with Ford during this time of mourning.

INDEX

ABOUT THE AUTHOR

Donn P. Werling has been director of the National Historic Landmark home of Henry Ford (which is owned and operated by the University of Michigan) since 1983. During that time. he has met and interviewed dozens of former Ford associates, relatives, servants, and friends—not only at the Estate but at all six of Ford's principal winter, summer, and fall residences.

Werling earned his Ph.D. from the University of Michigan, and he holds graduate degrees from Michigan State University and Loyola of Chicago, and his undergraduate degree is from Valparaiso University. Werling served for four years on the Alumni Advisory Board to the Honors College, one of the premiere honors colleges in the country, and he has been named to Marquis' *Who's Who in America* since 1995.

Werling has taught, created, published, and presented heritage educational materials to hundreds of audiences—from university students to elementary-school-aged children to elderhostels. In 1994, Werling won the External Service Award from the University of Michigan–Dearborn. He has composed almost a dozen songs about Henry Ford, most of which have been performed in a school musicale entitled *Henry Ford and His Uncommon Friends*. Werling's first book in 1973 was published by the State of Illinois and the Open Lands project, and it won the Russell Wilson prize from the School of Education of the University of Michigan in Ann Arbor. Werling's 1989 audio tape later accompanied by a songbook, *Lakes and Lighthouses*, won a national award at the annual meeting of the National Association for Interpretation of our nation's heritage. Werling's most recent publication was *Uncommon Friends of an Uncommon Century*, a companion piece to the musicale, published by the Center for Heritage Education of the University of Michigan, with a grant from the Charles Edison Fund.

Werling founded the Henry Ford Heritage Association and co-founded the Automobile National Heritage Area. He co-chaired the organizing committee for many years. Legislation creating this area was passed in 1998 by both houses of the U.S. Congress and signed by President William Clinton in November of that year. It is the first U.S. national park to interpret the most sweeping innovation of the twentieth century: the introduction of the automobile.